Jennifer Day is a parent coach and counsellor with more than twenty-five years of experience, having worked in the field of emotional intelligence since its inception. Originally a choreographer and professional dance teacher, she spent nine years studying alternative approaches to the mastering of emotions and stress on both sides of the Atlantic. The resulting Applied Emotional Mastery® (a practical methodology for managing stress in parents and children and building emotional and social intelligence) has been the subject of studies internationally and has been coached and taught to thousands of individuals, executives, physicians, students, teachers and parents in the US and the UK. She is the bestselling author of *Creative Visualization with Children: A Practical Guide* and *Children Believe Everything You Say*, as well as other books.

INTUITIVE PARENTING

Jennifer Day

A How To book

ROBINSON

ROBINSON

First published in Great Britain in 2019 by Robinson

13 5 7 9 10 8 6 4 2

Copyright © Jennifer Day, 2019

A CIP catalogue record for this book
is available from the British Library.

ISBN: 978-1-47214-218-4

Typeset in Whitman by Hewer Text UK Ltd, Edinburgh
Printed and bound in Great Britain by Clays Ltd, Elcograf S.p.A.

Papers used by Robinson are from well-managed forests and other responsible sources.

Robinson
An imprint of
Little, Brown Book Group
Carmelite House
50 Victoria Embankment
London EC4Y 0DZ

An Hachette UK Company
www.hachette.co.uk

www.littlebrown.co.uk

How To Books are published by Robinson, an imprint of Little, Brown Book
Group. We welcome proposals from authors who have first-hand experience
of their subjects. Please set out the aims of your book, its target market and
its suggested contents in an email to howtobooks@littlebrown.co.uk.

INTUITIVE PARENTING

For
Ella and Mara

Contents

Introduction

'It is easier to build strong children than to repair broken men.' Attributed to Frederick Douglass (c. 1850s)

WHY WE HAVE LOST TOUCH WITH OUR PARENTING INTUITION AND HOW WE CAN REGAIN IT

In this time of numerous parenting experts offering vastly differing views on every imaginable aspect of child-rearing, the consequence among busy, overworked and often over-extended parents is self-conscious, Google-driven, fretful-to-the-point-of-being-calculated parenting. Children experience their parents' over-anxious, preoccupied concern, and themselves develop anxiety and an insecure sense of self. Parenting intuition, both as a concept and an innate ability, has for the past few decades become undermined if not usurped by the thousands of parenting books, blogs and so-called parenting experts flooding the market. But raising a child 'by the book' or according to the directives of a shedload of 'experts' (including me) is like trying to live a healthy life by following every diet trend; Paleo, Atkins, macrobiotic and raw-food diets (to name just a few) have all intermittently been hailed as the greatest diet ever and then, after a while, their limitations become apparent. The intention may be good, but ultimately making any significant choices in our lives by following trends can have inadvertent and unhappy consequences.

Loving, caring parents who are sincerely committed to doing the best for their children are self-consciously, and often anxiously, trying to follow advice that is regularly contradictory and frequently also encourages them to be alert for symptoms of a pathology or disorder. Diagnostics has, of course, helped countless children and families handle great challenges and traumas. Increasing numbers of psychologists and mental health professionals, however, are becoming concerned about the over-diagnosis of too many children, as well as the mounting angst in parents contributing to over-anxiety in their children and the disturbing rise in mental health problems among ever younger children.

For the average child, increased diagnosis is not the answer. Nor is blaming or turning to schools or necessarily even 'experts'. The ever-speeding roller-coaster ride we are on of excessive cognitive analysis and hyper advice-giving is not working – instead, it is leading to analysis paralysis: we are losing touch with our innate human needs and abilities, our need to connect *in person* and our ability to tune in to each other and to ourselves and our own intuition. In my view, this applies as much if not more to parents and children than any other group.

Throughout decades of working with families, teachers, parents and children, I have seen over and over again that meeting this innate need and ability to connect and tune in requires not more advice but less; it requires simplification and letting go of the over-emphasis on expert advice, labelling and analysis; and it requires us 'professionals' to step back, impose less and listen more. It requires that we turn towards the parents and empower them to access and draw on their own wisdom; to give them information instead of advice, and knowledge rather than analysis. Giving parents an understanding of *why* real connection and tuning in to yourselves and your children (and showing how) is critical in my view, the only way to regain parental self-confidence.

Multiple decades of experience have taught me that, whether you are a parent, grandparent or child-caregiver, you are highly likely to have an intuitive wisdom that can help you raise the children in your care with much less anxiety and stress about 'doing it right' than has become the norm. I have witnessed countless parents become empowered and confident after gaining basic knowledge about how the brain-body-behaviour connection works, and how to use that knowledge to reconnect with their own parenting insights and intuition.

I have written this book with that fact in mind, and also with the acute awareness that most parents have no time to read a thick book with protracted information where they have to spend time searching for the aspect that's relevant to them. The book is deliberately short and, I hope, to the point, with practical tools you can apply immediately, all expressing the idea that if you are coherent and tuned in to yourself, your child and your intuition, you will access the wisest expert either of you could find. Being tuned in to your intuition will give you insights and perspectives that are specific to you and that show you how to apply the knowledge you glean to your parenting, without anxiety or feeling overwhelmed.

As you read the book, you will become increasingly familiar with how to tune in to your intuition and intuitive wisdom at will and, I hope, recognise their elements (and power) as something you have really known all along! But in order to build your confidence in this innate state, you must first address the reasons why you are not already there, or what is getting in the way of you sustaining it.

Much like approaching a garden you may want to enhance and enrich, or a computer you want to clean and upgrade, you need to approach yourself and your own development as a natural 'work in progress', and recognise that you, like all of us, have developed parent anxieties and stress-induced issues that – like weeds in a garden or old programs on a laptop – need replacing or upgrading. Once 'downloaded' and integrated, the tuned-in approach will become part of your way of life, and a more confident and loving connection with your child will ultimately ensue.

The difference between intuition and instinct

Finally, before we move on I want to clarify the difference, as I see it, between intuition and instinct. The two terms are often used interchangeably and this failure to differentiate them can lead us to think they are the same thing. Because both our intuition and instinct seem to appear out of nowhere and we don't know how or why we feel what we feel, it is easy to confuse the two. I believe, however, that there is a distinct difference, which is especially relevant to parenting, and they each serve a different purpose.

Instinct is a biologically hardwired survival mechanism. It is designed to help us sense danger or warning signs of threat and is often connected to our 'fight or flight' response. Because we are not equipped to be consciously alert to all dangers, risks or hazards, our instinct works with all our physical senses and our subconscious to signal to us when we need to be on our guard or extra vigilant. Our conscious mind can only take in and process fewer than two hundred stimuli simultaneously, whereas our subconscious – greatly assisted by our limbic system and its stored experiences– can process many millions per second, and herein lies our instinctive capacity.

If we 'have a feeling' that a certain path our teenager is pursuing could be dodgy or even perilous, our instinct may be warning us with feelings of apprehension, unease or judgement. Or, if we are walking alone at night and have a gut feeling that someone is following us even though we can't see or hear anything, that is usually our instinct alerting us, and our accompanying fear will activate the appropriate 'fight or flight' response.

Intuition, on the other hand, signals us through what is deeply impor-tant to us, through feelings of unconditional love, balanced care and being 'in flow', and often is in alignment with our values and our desired direction of growth. It does not tend to function in stress but rather when we are completely present and 'in the now'. Intuition can be described as our 'north star' that doesn't necessarily show us why a particular direction is the right one; we 'just know' – it 'feels right'.

As a parent, your intuition is that inner conviction you have that your child needs a certain experience or connection, and you have little or no way of explaining why; you 'just know'. You may even feel there is a step that needs to be taken although you don't know the step that follows it – this first step 'feels right, in your heart'. It is a sense of knowing that most of the time we cannot explain. If we trust and follow our intuition, inevitably it turns out to be a good or right decision. The key here is trust – trusting our intuition requires recognising it first, then having the confidence to act on it.

When our instinct alerts us, it is important to pay attention to it for obvious reasons. Physically it will feel uncomfortable, like a nagging or uneasy feeling in the stomach that, if danger is present, needs to be acted on. When there is no evidence of immediate threat, however, there is a chance that the instinct could be based on memories or unresolved emotions from a similar situation, so it might be prudent to also engage the intuition before acting.

The intuition, in contrast, tends to feel subtler, like a nudge or an urge that you can't explain, and a sense of calm clarity that can also register as a sensation or stirring in the stomach and heart area. Developing discernment between the two is like learning two different languages, and requires first and foremost increased self-awareness, mentally, emotionally and physically.

I hope by the time you've finished reading this book you'll have gained both the knowledge and tools to do just that – and that you'll have increased your connection to your intuition, most particularly your parenting intuition, and be well on the way to building more trust in it, with more confidence in your parenting as a result.

In view of the very busy lives of parents today, each chapter in the book has been kept short, and contains some practical tips to help you integrate the information from that chapter – all tips and suggestions leading towards building and strengthening your parent intuition. Occasionally, I have supplied references or recommendations for further reading as footnotes on the relevant page, should you want to explore further any of the concepts or research presented. But, most importantly, I encourage you to put the concepts into practice!

Chapter 1

What Every Parent Should Know (But Doesn't) About the Brain

> *'Early experience shapes the structure and function of the brain. This reveals the fundamental way in which gene expression is determined by experience.'* Daniel J. Siegel, *The Developing Mind* (Guilford Press, 1999)

PLASTICITY AND HOW THE BRAIN CHANGES

Let's begin with some basic facts about what makes us behave and connect – or disconnect – as parents and children, as humans. After more than a century of discussion about the 'Nature versus Nurture' concept, it has finally been established that the way a child grows into adulthood is determined largely by, not *either* nature or nurture, but both DNA *and* the environment – the influence of caregivers. Most recently, a few decades of neuro-scientific research findings show us that the brain is actually changeable and has what the scientists call plasticity, meaning that the brain's structure continually changes, not just in the growing child but throughout life.* Exactly how it changes depends on our

---

* Daniel J. Siegel, *The Developing Mind* (Guilford Press, 1999); Daniel J. Siegel and Tina Payne Bryson, *The Whole Brain Child* (Delacorte Press, 2011).

experiences – emotional, mental and physical – and our responses to those experiences.

This discovery of the brain's plasticity alters age-old beliefs about growth and human potential (which used to espouse that brains stopped developing at twenty-something and it was downhill after that). The new discoveries make wonderful news for us adults, because it means we can be more confident in our capacity to learn, grow and make changes in behaviours, although if we have children in our lives, the knowledge that their young brains are also physically and structurally impacted by all their experiences can be a sobering thought – and just a tad of pressure. Of course, there are many other factors involved in children's brain growth, including mental stimulation, physical activity, social interaction, and the basic ingredients of diet, sleep and safety, as well as the DNA – inherited genetics, and epigenetics (the expression of the genes based on factors like the environment and social stimulation).

THE BRAIN'S 'THREAT SYSTEM'

The brain and its behaviour can be one of the most important aspects of a child's upbringing for parents to consider, not just because of the obvious developmental stages of the child's brain, but also because of the parent's own brain, and how it impacts parenting behaviour.

Most of us don't think about our brains and how they work, or are even aware that the brain is made up of several parts, each with roles to play. For example, the part of the brain that has ensured our survival as a species throughout the ages is known as the limbic system, and is often referred to as the emotional brain because it is responsible for processing and expressing strong emotions. One of its primary functions is to receive information from all of our senses – sight, sound, smell, taste, touch – in order to make an evaluation about whether we are safe or threatened and in need of defending ourselves.

How we determine what exactly is threatening is largely due to the two parts of the limbic system called the amygdala and the hippocampus, each with different roles remembering and storing – or coding in the main – what we perceive as threatening, much of which is established throughout childhood. In simple terms, the amygdala is responsible for recognising the signals that activate your perception of strong emotional, often sub-conscious threat, for example the fear someone might have felt as a child as a result of being bitten by a dog, and their resulting anxiety around dogs. The hippocampus, on the other hand, stores more of the factual memory or conscious context within which your emotional memories exist, which in this example could include the shape and size of the dog's head, or the type of dog, and being pulled away by a parent.

This limbic system encompasses the only system we have to respond to threat, whether it's a real physical threat, such as the example above, or a threat to the ego (such as being ignored in a conversation, or a text not responded to), or a threat in the part of the brain that worries about the future (such as getting a red light when you're running late).

THE 'THINKING' BRAIN

While the limbic system is extremely powerful and significant, it occupies only a small space, near the base of the brain between the ears.

Most of the human skull is occupied by the largest part of the brain called the neo-cortex, which contains all the parts that make us uniquely human. This includes centres that give us our ability for empathy, curiosity, language, abstract thinking, strategising, problem solving, creativity and creative expression, integration and much more.

While the limbic system is somewhat developed at birth, recent research shows that the neo-cortex is not, and in fact does not fully mature until about the age of twenty-four. Throughout childhood, as the neo-cortex or 'thinking' part of the brain is being constructed and developing, so too is the storehouse of information in the 'emotional brain' – the amygdala and the hippocampus – for what constitutes threat.

If, based on childhood experiences and conditioning, the limbic system perceives an event as a threat, the neo-cortex – or logical, reasoning part of the brain – is, regardless of its size, effectively bypassed. This is because in a situation of real physical threat, you need all your focus and energy to fight or run away (fight or flight), and qualities such as curiosity and empathy would not be appropriate (you wouldn't want to be considering whether the bear chasing you was a brown or a black bear).

When the 'fight or flight' system is triggered, 'threat instructions' are sent straight to the body (heart, stomach, lungs) where systems that do not help in handling danger (including the digestive system and the brain's empathic and creative centres) start to shut down to divert energy to the systems needed for action like running away or fighting.

Although in the case of a red light you may know that you are not really under physical threat, if you have a strong emotional reaction to the red light, the speed of this 'threat system' means it is triggered before your logical thinking interrupts it.

This is the cause of unhelpful and damaging stress responses (more on this later). Only when you are able to manage your emotional reactions can you take charge of such a response, which involves engaging several parts of the neo-cortex.

How we hardwire children's brains

In children, however, the necessary centres of the brain are not developed enough to be able to manage their emotions. In fact, throughout childhood their brains undergo a colossal and on-going construction, followed by adolescence and the teenage years when an extensive remodelling occurs that lasts well into adulthood. So, while it is difficult for adults to respond to stressful situations with managed, balanced choices, for children it is substantially more difficult. I would go so far as to say it is unreasonable to expect them to do the same with a brain that has far from developed the necessary capacity.

This basic information about the brain is critically important for parents and child-care givers to understand, especially because the areas of the brain responsible for emotions – strong and otherwise – in particular change in response to experiences, and the changes are strengthened by repeated experience.

For example, recurrent focus on what we don't have or aren't doing right strengthens our negative 'default' neural pathways in the brain, just as we strengthen the 'positive' pathways when we focus on the positive aspects of life or whatever we enjoy. Whichever emotional pathways in the brain we strengthen will become more dominant. If they are negative, they make it more difficult for us to make the changes we want. Conversely, if they are positive, they will increase our ability to focus on what we want to achieve.

Practically, this means that our brains are continuously being wired and rewired, or, using a computer metaphor, our brains are continuously being updated and new software is being regularly downloaded. For adults, this is akin to upgrading but, for children, it's more like hardwiring. The good news about this is that once you understand some basic details about children's and parents' brain functions and the associated emotional needs, you can begin to create conditions that make connections and positive outcomes a lot more likely, and throughout the chapters in this book I will be offering some practical tools and simple skills to help.

Chapter 2

There But Not There

'Children contend with parents who are physically close, tantalisingly so, but mentally elsewhere.' Sherry Turkle, *Alone Together: Why We Expect More from Technology and Less from Each Other* (Basic Books, 2011)

PARENTS' GREATEST FEAR

I like to address 'what gets in the way', or, to put it bluntly, the worst pain points, as early as possible because this usually overshadows any and all concerns that parents have, so resolving it is of benefit to other issues, whether directly or indirectly. So here goes: what is the greatest fear parents have today?

You might think it's terrorism, or the fear that their children will be less financially secure than they themselves are. Maybe you think it's online bullying or future education opportunities. At one time, it may have been job opportunities or job security, or the lack of either, or maybe unsafe sex or drugs. It could actually be any of these things, and probably is at one time or another for most parents. Statistically, however, the one thing that most parents today consistently report dreading is that their children will show signs of or develop mental health problems, and it's really not surprising.

Almost every day we read or hear about worrying trends of increasing emotional and mental health issues among children. Online and in every area of the media we are inundated with reports about the escalating problems in young people, ranging from anxiety and depression, to coping and relationship issues, many of which are so severe that basic functioning is difficult.

Widely published surveys give an alarming picture: for example, in the UK, an NHS and Department of Education study reported a 285 per cent increase in children treated for self-harm, and a 172 per cent increase in children treated for eating disorders. In the USA, an alarming and steady increase in child suicides and suicidal ideation has been reported by the Pediatric Academic Societies, and according to the US National Institute of Mental Health more than 30 per cent of girls and 20 per cent of boys suffer from an anxiety disorder. According to the American Psychology Association, 95 per cent of surveyed college counselling directors reported that the number of students with 'significant psychological problems is a growing concern', and a recent UK YouGov survey showed that a third of UK students reported suffering from mental health problems. Several recent studies are showing that children as young as four are suffering from anxiety, panic attacks and depression.

What's going on?

WHY THE LOSS OF 'THE VILLAGE' IS DETRIMENTAL TO CHILDREN

Aside from the children diagnosed with clinical mental health conditions or serious learning difficulties who, of course, require medical treatment, I have seen enough evidence in my parent-coaching practice as well as in conversations with colleagues and therapists that convince me there is something else going on.

The disturbing numbers we see include many healthy children who are developing anxiety, attention difficulties and emotional challenges well on the way to becoming pathologies that are, in my mind, completely needless.

Among family therapists, social workers and other professionals interacting with these issues on a daily basis, there is a growing consensus that a new kind of intense and precarious emotional fragility exists among young people that hasn't been evident before.

There are differing opinions as to the root cause, but evidence seems to suggest that three factors are involved, the first one being a collapse of 'the village it takes to raise a child'. This has nothing to do with parents not caretaking or caring enough – in fact, quite the opposite – but I'll get back to that shortly. It has to do with a series of events and factors which include the weakening of the social contexts that used to sustain and reinforce family and parental support systems needed for healthy emotional development; these included extended family members in relatively close vicinity, tightly knit communities where everyone knew the neighbourhood children, and community support organisations such as churches and community centres. All of these provided the necessary 'tribe' of adults for children to turn to, and all have been declining over recent decades.

How social media affects children's emotional growth

This loss of the 'village' and community – often exacerbated by the growth in divorced and one-parent families – has created a vacuum that has been filled by the escalation of technology and, in particular, social media with the 24/7 influence of popular culture and peer group pressures that it enables.

Although a growing body of evidence shows how damaging screen time in itself can be for children (that's a whole other book),* it is the replacement of the 'village' by social media (and media generally) that is most disconcerting and is the most relevant to intuitive parenting. This is particularly because it has been undermining and in many cases completely usurping family influence and parental authority, along with the emotional security that these relationships, in their best incarnation, bring.

In addition to all the social media activity, another indication of this is that children are becoming increasingly familiar with characters in the media, often to the point where they are more attached to them than to real people. Because such characters can be accessed through one media or another at just about any time, they can easily end up taking the place of critical human relational interactions necessary for both brain growth and social and emotional development. The neural pathways that need to develop for children to mature into

---

* For more information, look for policy statements and research articles by the National Association for the Education of Young Children (NAEYC) and the American Academy of Pediatrics, research papers from University College London and King's College London, and publications such as *Psychology Today*.

socially well-functioning and resilient adults require actual face-to-face interactions, multiple times a day. Gradually, the experiences provided by these interactions develop their ability for appropriate, instant (non-edited) responses to others' facial and body-language cues, as well as variation in speech.

The sensitivity to more subtle communication as well as empathic skills is also a part of this process, and the development of these vital neural pathways and associated skills takes time and repetition – endless repetition. The time lost to media and interactivity through screens is sadly not time that can be regained.

PARENTS' IT USE AND HOW IT IMPACTS CHILDREN'S EMOTIONAL NEEDS

But the problem is not just down to the children's use of screens and social media. In fact, as the second of the three causes I suggest, misuse of technology actually includes parents as much as, if not more than, their children, with their own often excessive use of texting and social media.

In one of the earliest studies looking into this question, researcher and MIT Professor Sherry Turkle initially focused on children's 'addiction' to their phones but soon discovered that an unforeseen and more significant issue was the breakdown of parent–child communication due to parents' distracted texting.[*] Younger children

---

[*] Sherry Turkle, *Alone Together: Why We Expect More from Technology and Less from Each Other* (Basic Books, 2011); Sherry Turkle, 'Always-on/Always-on-You: The Tethered Self', in Katz, James E. (ed.), *Handbook of Mobile Communication Studies* (MIT Press, 2008).

reported feeling as if they had to compete with their parents' devices for their attention, and Turkle observed that 'Children today are being deprived of important conversations with their parents due to the disruptions of technology.' Author of the 2015 book *Reclaiming Conversation: The Power of Talk in a Digital Age*, Turkle has dedicated her professional life to studying the effects of technology on human interaction: 'What I'm seeing is parents who are not stepping up to the importance of mentoring, and to the conversations that will create empathy and a capacity for solitude in their children.' In other words, parents are not recognising their own significance in their children's lives.

Although parents may well be spending time *in the presence* of their children, being physically with them, they are often too busy to be *genuinely fully present* with them, or as one eight-year-old put it to me, 'She is there but she's not there.'

Sadly, the technological innovations that were, and are, meant to transform our world in such positive ways are instead, along with information overload, undermining our ability and need to interact directly with real human beings as well as our ability to focus on anything for any length of time, including our children. The result is a generation of young adults who have been raised with fragmented, distracted attention from their parents. For the next generation, it appears to be escalating even further, with children feeling unable to rely on their parents' focused loving interest, and never getting their critical emotional needs completely met, so they don't have what family therapists call 'secure attachment'. This describes those crucial moments of attachment needed to develop feelings of emotional safety which are the basis for future healthy relationships. Such moments of potential attachment are now being cut short by sudden redirection to a text, tweet, message or another distraction.

To further provoke the situation, parents often hand their smartphones or other devices to their youngsters to keep them entertained or occupied, leading to children who are at risk of developing a 'secure attachment' to their devices rather than to their parents (who may have already developed an attachment to theirs).

Our ubiquitous and ever-growing attachment to our smartphones also results in a less obvious issue, which is the ease of access to each other that this gives us. While this is mostly a very useful thing – children's use of their own phone can be beneficial in many situations (including for emergency or safety reasons) – it can also lead to them turning far too quickly to their parents for help or advice, rather than trying to solve problems themselves or relying on their own resourcefulness.

THE CHALLENGES OF OVER-PARENTING

Which brings me to the third key factor that appears to be increasing anxiety in children, and which we see manifesting especially so widely in college students: over-parenting – otherwise known as helicopter parenting. You might ask, is it possible to over-parent? If you love your child, surely you should want to do as much as you can, take care of them as much as possible? Yet it turns out that many parents are 'taking care' of their children far too much, in fact so much that the children are not developing the necessary coping skills and self-reliance they need to become functioning adults. Parents are forgetting the importance of individuation – and resilience.

However well-meaning, over-involved parents who keep children on a tight schedule of activities and school work, even if the desire is to ensure the best education and future success, are not allowing their children the time, space or responsibilities to individuate into confident self-reliance. Succumbing to the pressure of feeling that your children need to keep up, get ahead, advance up the ladder, outdo the competition, to be the best, causes the perceptions that lead to over-parenting and the resulting insecure, troubled, anxious children. All the well-intentioned, love-fuelled attempts by parents to guide, supervise and direct children towards success, results not only in achievement-pressure on the children but also actually prevents them from building the coping skills and resilience they will need to handle adult life and, ironically, that very pressure they are under!

In universities on both sides of the Atlantic we are seeing evidence of this – a generation of young people entering adult life who are unable to manage the basics of self-reliance, who have little or no resilience to bounce back after setbacks, rejection or disappointments, and who are suffering alarming levels of anxiety and stress-reactions to the simplest of everyday events. One UK study found that a third of first-year university students cannot do everyday tasks such as boiling an egg or their own laundry. The American College Health Association surveyed 100,000 students in over 50 universities and found that 84 per cent of them felt unable to cope.

No matter how much you plan their lives and protect them, your children will have to face challenges – on their own. To coin a phrase, *shit happens*. Your most important job as a parent is to teach your children how to handle 'the shit'. This means, of course, allowing them to fall and fail, just like you allowed them to fall and get up when they were learning to walk – again and again, without (I hope!) being subjected to judgement or being 'rescued'. That's how they learned to walk.

HOW TO OVERCOME THE FACTORS THAT UNDERMINE THE PARENT–CHILD CONNECTION

All three factors I have mentioned – the loss of the 'village', the adverse impact of digital technology and over-parenting – are linked, and the thread that ties them together is the need for real connection: not the technology-driven connection that requires a device, but the three-dimensional human connection between parent and child, the connection that occurs when a parent is fully present with themselves and with their child, and tuned in to themselves as well as to their child.

As technological advances are coming at us with the speed of a runaway train, and many of those advances are becoming more and more necessary for the way we function, we need to prioritise and commit to *fully present and tuned-in parenting* in order to create a balance, and provide an emotionally secure and healthy childhood for our children that they otherwise will not have. It is a simple concept, although maybe not always easy. Throughout this book, I will attempt to give you a practical guide to what that *tuned-in parenting with presence* really looks like, how it is the expression of our parenting intuition and how you can achieve it practically, in everyday life.

To begin, here are a few steps you can take to better control your screen habits and to become more fully present with yourself and your child:

1. Each morning upon waking, before checking your phone or any other device, stretch and take a deep breath. Then allow a long exhale as you relax your body and any tension from your sleeping positions. Now think of one thing you can really appreciate about your child. Connect to the feeling it gives you or just the feeling of love for your little one. Place a hand on your chest or over your heart and really feel that good feeling of appreciation and love. Really feel the feeling, physically. Allow yourself to smile before you move on with your day.

2. Eliminate all screens from your bedrooms – and from the children's bedrooms. The most obvious reason for this is that while looking at our screens we are preventing the production of melatonin, the chemical our brain releases that is necessary for sleep. Normally melatonin is produced as it gets dark, giving us a wind-down experience and readying us for sleep. When we stare at the blue light on our screens that production is delayed or interrupted. Adults need seven to nine hours of sleep in order for the brain's neurons to fully rest and 'reconfigure', and for the supportive glial cells to release all the day's toxins completely so we can function most effectively the next day. For the same

reason, children need between ten and twelve hours a night depending on their age, to ensure the necessary neural growth also takes place. So, for children's developing brains, screen time at night is particularly damaging.

3. Remove devices from the dining table – all meals should be without screens. Focus on each other and on face-to-face conversations. If you find prioritising this difficult, imagine yourself for a moment on your deathbed: will you be regretting that you didn't spend more time checking your phone or not giving more focused attention to your child?

4. When your children are speaking to you (i.e. when you pick them up from school), put your phone away. Make a habit of looking into your child's eyes when having a conversation. To bring yourself into the present-moment awareness that this requires, take a deep breath and, as you exhale, focus your attention in your chest, sensing your heart in the centre of your breath. Place a hand on your chest if necessary, and feel the connection to yourself, and to your child.

5. If you are waiting to meet your child, instead of checking your phone, place your hands in your lap and close your eyes for one minute. Take your focused attention down into one hand, noting the temperature and sensations in your hand and fingers. Do the same with your other hand. Then with both hands simultaneously. Then allow that attention to travel up your arms to your heart. Connect with the feeling of love you have for your child. Open your eyes. Hold the good feeling. Greet your child with it.

6. Think of how you address a colleague or your doctor or bank manager. It is likely that you give them your full and present attention. Pick one time during the day when you commit to yourself to meet your child with the same full presence and focused attention. Your children will remember for the rest of their life that they were important enough for you to switch off technology and connect with and listen to them.

Chapter 3

Your Three Levels of Influence

'There is no parent more vulnerable to over-parenting that an
unhappy parent. One of the most important things we can do for
our children is to present them with a version of adult life that
is appealing and worth striving for.' Madeline Levine, 'Raising
Successful Children', *New York Times* (4 August 2012)

HOW IMPORTANT IS A PARENT'S INFLUENCE?

As we delve into intuitive parenting and look at how we can tune into
our intuition more consistently and act on it with more confidence,
we need to include and address all that gets in the way of it. Intuitive
parenting is, after all, the most natural thing in the world, so accessing, trusting and drawing on it is more about removing obstacles than
it is about learning anything new. In fact, I would posit that nothing I
suggest in this book will be anything you don't already know on some
level – except possibly some of the research and scientific information that backs it up. Of all the obstacles I have witnessed and experienced that get in the way of intuitive parenting, one stands out the
most: the misapprehension parents have of their own power.

Parents are the most important people in a child's life. This is not
news. We are all aware of the significant role parents or primary

caregivers play, but we don't seem to be equally aware of the multiple levels and degrees of influence we, as parents, have on our offspring. Children listen, absorb and believe everything their parents and teachers say. As they grow older they may not listen as well or believe *everything* grown-ups say, but they still absorb it, and it shapes their reality and the way they interact with others. If there was shouting or verbal abuse in our home growing up, it almost certainly taught us that this is an appropriate form of communication. If there was chaos, confusion and lack of management in our home or school, it may have given us the belief that adults are incapable of effective direction, in which case we probably sought direction from peers instead.

Children also absorb – and sometimes even take literally – abusive language that is not necessarily meant to be abusive. For example, 'Are you stupid or something?!' or 'You never get it right!' or 'Stop being such a pain!' Any of these types of exclamations will give the child messages that make them feel emotionally unsafe and of little worth. Repeated, such verbal attacks can contribute to low self-esteem and low self-expectations, and often have far-reaching effects on the child's life and relationships well into adulthood.

This immense influence we who raise children have on the young ones in our care is at the core of 'tuned-in' intuitive parenting, and it is central to the nature of every child and how their future unfolds. Yet this highly consequential influence is something that most of us only briefly think about and, in many cases, have difficulty taking responsibility for.

Overwhelmed as we often are by the practical demands of our parenting role, relationships and jobs, juggling financial responsibilities with professional desires or ambitions, and the demands of over-connected social lives (whether on- or offline), the responsibility of our influence on our child's brain development and emotional health can appear daunting and even too exhausting to contemplate.

The challenges facing parents, caregivers, teachers and grandparents today are probably greater than at any other time in history. Never before have we had to raise and educate children exposed to the uncharted influences, excessive stimulation and constant state of worldwide flux. Greater uncertainty exists within our society and throughout the world today. It is not surprising many feel overwhelmed. The paradox is that our influence, the conscious influence of parents, is probably more vital for our children's future than ever before.

THE THREE LEVELS OF PARENTAL INFLUENCE

In essence, we influence our children on three levels:

1. with what we *say*;
2. with what we *do* and *model* or *demonstrate*;
3. with what we *feel*.

Most of us can recognise that if what we *say* isn't consistent with what we *do*, we create confusion and incoherence. In other words, we know that the old maxim 'Do as I say, not as I do!' is obsolete and doesn't work. Whatever we say to a child needs to be followed up by action that is congruent with our spoken words. If not, children lose respect – with often dire consequences.

As if this isn't challenging enough, there is a third element that we need to take into consideration, which is how we *feel*. If what we feel is inconsistent with either of the other two, insecurities and a sense of inauthenticity will begin to permeate the parent–child relationship – as it actually will do any relationship whether it is with your partner, spouse or any other family member or friends. When it happens in a parent–child relationship, however, it is more acute: children are considerably more sensitive to the effect created by our emotional state than adults are. The key is consistency between all three modes of 'communication' or influence.

THE SIGNIFICANCE OF WHAT WE SAY TO CHILDREN

Most adults' emotional states today are controlled by internal self-talk and what-ifs: 'What if I get ill?'; 'What if I can't pay the bills?'; 'What if I was seen speeding through the red light?' Without much examination, when our children are very young we teach them to do the same. We conjure up images, in detail, to keep them from getting hurt or to enforce discipline: 'Be careful or you'll fall and hurt yourself!'; 'If you're not careful a car will run you over and you'll have to go to hospital!'; 'If you don't study for this test, you'll fail and then what will become of you? You'll . . . . .!' (Please feel free to fill in the blank space.) Unfortunately, we do not spend nearly as much time or attention on giving our children, or ourselves, positive self-talk and internal images.

We all say things such as 'I'm sick to death of it!', 'He's a pain in the neck!', 'I've just about reached boiling point!' and 'You'll be the death of me!' How do our own internal images and what-ifs impact the way we talk to our children, never mind what it does to our children's imaginations, and especially to little ones who still take what we say literally? (Imagine for a moment what might go on in a toddler's mind when they hear their mother say, 'I need this like a hole in the head!')

Although it's usually well-intentioned, much of the imagery we project onto our children is fear-based. Because we want to protect them we say things such as 'Don't run in the road – you'll get run over!', 'Watch out, you'll hurt yourself!' and so on. Then there are the threats we make, such as 'If you don't stop jumping up and down I will never bring you here again!' or 'If you do that one more time we're not going to Disneyworld, ever!' These types of threats are unlikely to be followed through, which will only result in children not taking us seriously and ultimately losing respect for our authority.

It doesn't have to be that way, however: we don't have to resort to these emotionally driven outbursts. We can change the way we express ourselves to a more positive, mindful but still effective way of communicating. This all begins with being more self-aware, tuned in to ourselves and consequently our intuition and our child. It may take time and practice, but seeing the difference it can make to our children makes it well worth the effort, and we can start by becoming aware of our own language.

Try this:

Read the following list of *negative remarks* and suggested positive alternatives.

> *Watch out or you'll fall and hurt yourself!*
>
> Hold tight and you'll be safe. / Notice how those steps are wet and slippery.
>
> *Why are you being so difficult?!*
>
> I can see you're not feeling happy. Let's talk about it. / Tell me what's going on for you.
>
> *What are you doing – are you stupid!?*
>
> Maybe that's not such a good idea? Let's explore how you can do that differently
>
> *You'll never get that right! You're just too clumsy!*
>
> I know you can get it right if you keep trying – let me know if you need any help!

Now try to come up with your own alternatives for the following:

> *You're driving me crazy!*
>
> *You're so lazy, you'll never get anywhere!*
>
> *That's going to end in tears!*
>
> *What's wrong with you? Why can't you behave?*

How did that go? My own alternatives (with imagined scenarios) were . . .

You're driving me crazy!

I am having a hard time with your behaviour. Let's stop and take a few breaths and start again.

You're so lazy. You'll never get anywhere!

I am confident you can do better. What would help you try a bit harder?

That's going to end in tears!

Dolls are for playing with, not fighting. Put it back in the toy-box please.

What's wrong with you? Why can't you behave?

Looks like you have some big feelings going on. Let's go outside and you can tell me about it.

The most beneficial way to use this exercise is to take some quiet time to make your own list of negative remarks and see if you can find a positive way to re-phrase each one. Team up with a friend or your partner and keep a notebook of each other's language for one week. Jot down all negative and fear-based language you hear your partner using. At the end of the week, get together and compare notes. Discuss how you can best help each other to adjust to more positive phrasing. Once your awareness increases, involve your children too. Ask them for suggestions on how to improve phrasing, and look for ways to improve family language awareness. Make it a team effort. Avoid lecturing or 'telling' your children – after all, much of their negative language was probably picked up from you or another adult.

Once your awareness of your language is heightened, it will help you increase your awareness of how congruent your words are with your actions, i.e. how they come together as one and give the same message – or NOT, as the case may be. Awareness is everything!

How what we do and demonstrate
impacts our children

All children are affected by the congruence or incongruence of the adults in their lives – by whether we practise what we preach or 'walk the talk'. If we expect our children to be kind, it follows that we must show them what kindness is. If we would like our children to have a sense of purpose and to feel passionate about something, we ourselves must be able to demonstrate what it looks like to have a sense of purpose and feel passionate about something in our lives. If we want our children to be 'life learners', we can only facilitate that by being continuously open to learning on our own life journey. And if we ask our children to manage their emotions and be who they authentically are, we ourselves have to know what that looks like and act accordingly.

Make a list of the behaviours that you believe are important for your child or children to embody. Once you have completed it, next to each behaviour note what might be getting in the way of you yourself behaving or acting that way. (For example, if you want your child to be polite, what gets in the way of *you* being polite to everyone you meet?)

Once you have completed this exercise, you will probably find that most things that get in the way of your ideal behaviours are things that you perceive as negative or stressful. When you perceive events as stressful or negative, your emotions are also negative – you may feel frustrated, disappointed, anxious, worried, fearful or angry. As we have already seen, and I am sure you have personally experienced, the result of this is often physical tension or ailments and usually behaviours that you later regret or wish you had done differently; the neo-cortex or 'thinking' brain – as I mentioned in the Introduction – becomes inhibited by the limbic system and emotional reaction, reduces our capacity to think clearly. This results in behaviour that is often not in line with our own belief system.

When this happens, we invariably feel judgement against ourselves, as well as possibly also feelings of guilt and other negative emotions, which in turn result in more stress – and the cycle begins again.

How parents' emotions influence children

To effectively interrupt this cycle, it helps first to understand the powerful force that underlies and perpetuates it all: when we take action, or behave in a certain way (for example raising our voice in anger), this behaviour is a result of a thought we have had, for example 'this child is out of line and I need to stop him now', or of a belief, for example 'it is not acceptable for children to behave this way'. Underlying this belief or thought is a feeling such as embarrassment, irritation, anxiety or fear of losing control of the situation. This feeling is driven by an emotion in the body (a turbulent or negative sensation, often experienced in the chest or the gut), which in turn can be attributed to physiology (increased/erratic heart rate, excessive stomach acid, shallow/erratic respiration). In other words, our emotions are actually shifts in energy,[*] moving through the body, which in turn affect our thinking and then determine our actions or behaviours.

Sometimes this cycle does not align with our beliefs or values, which adds another dimension to the negative emotions – usually feelings of unease, discomfort or a nagging sensation in the back of our minds.

In the above scenario, for example, we might believe that it is not acceptable for our child to behave in a certain way, but we may also have strong beliefs regarding violence and anger; we may believe that yelling at children is not appropriate. In that case, allowing ourselves to raise our voice in anger contradicts one belief while expressing another! Not only does this create confusion within our own mind, it also creates a lack of congruence towards our children, which leaves them also feeling at best confused.

Fortunately, this can be addressed and corrected without too much difficulty. In fact, I would posit that we are innately designed to

---

[*] Joseph LeDoux, *The Emotional Brain* (Simon & Schuster, 1996); J. LeDoux and R. Brown, 'A Higher Order Theory of Emotional Consciousness', *Proceedings of the National Academy of Sciences* (February 2017).

achieve congruence both in our communications and within ourselves because all our internal systems function at their best when we *are* congruent or, as it's also known, entrained.

Entrainment: What it is and why it is key to parental influence

Entrainment was identified back in the seventeenth century by the Dutch inventor of the pendulum clock, Christiaan Huygens, who discovered that, after he had set two of his pendulum clocks mounted next to each other swinging in different rhythms and in opposite directions, they became synchronised. He called this phenomenon 'coupled oscillators' and reported the results to the Royal Society (the UK's academy of science), referring to it as 'an odd kind of sympathy'.

This concept became known as entrainment and it has since been found to exist everywhere in nature, including within our own biology. A flock of geese entrains, as do schools of fish. Musical tuning forks entrain with each other when one tuning fork vibrates, and there are many other examples of entrainment between and using musical instruments,* including entire orchestras. You can see it in rowing teams and in dance, and in many other group activities where the people involved reach a state of being completely synchronised, moving as if they are one entity.

---

* Udo Will et al., 'Pulse and Entrainment to Non-Isochronous Auditory Stimuli', *PloS One* (7 April 2015).

Essentially entrainment is the synchronicity of several systems that otherwise function independently, achieved when all systems synchronise with the stronger of the systems. When entrainment occurs in the human body, the respiratory system, the autonomic nervous system, the digestive system and all other systems entrain with the most powerful organ (electrically) in the body, the heart. This occurs when we are in an emotionally positive, harmonious state of being, which is when the heart rhythms are coherent.[*]

Conversely, when we are in a state of stress or defensiveness and our heart rhythms are erratic, our brain and other biological systems become incoherent and internal chaos ensues, much like a school of fish being disrupted by the propeller of a boat. This process of entrainment versus incoherence also occurs in relationships *between* humans, the most well-researched example of which is between mother and baby.[†]

In any type of influential relationship, entrainment will occur proportionately to the 'leader' or strongest person's level of coherence. In other words, between parent and child, the parent's degree of internal, emotional coherence will likely determine the level of

[*] S. M. Morris, 'Achieving Collective Coherence: Group effects on Heart Rate Variability Coherence', *Alternative Therapies in Health; Medicine*, vol. 16, no. 4 (2010); R. McCraty, 'The Energetic Heart: Bioelectromagnetic Communication Within and Between People', in P. J. Rosch and M. S. Markov (eds), *Clinical Applications of Bioelectromagnetic Medicine* (Marcel Dekker, 2004).

[†] Ruth Feldman et al., 'Mother and Infant Coordinate Heart Rhythms through Episodes of Interaction Synchrony', *Infant Behavior and Development*, vol. 34, no. 4 (December 2011); Livio Provenzi, 'Mother–infant Dyadic Reparation', *Journal of Experimental Child Psychology*, vol. 140 (July 2015).

entrainment in the relationship; to what degree the child 'entrains' with the parent. The degree to which the parent is internally coherent will in turn depend on the congruence between what they say and do and feel.

HOW CHILDREN PICK UP PARENTAL AUTHENTICITY

As a child, I had my very own personal experience of this: my parents never argued or fought; neither did they show much affection towards each other. They were always civil, but I 'felt' that something was not right. When I was ten, I asked my mother but was told to 'stop being silly', that 'everything's fine'. Believing (as children do) that my parents were the ultimate authority I concluded that my feelings were wrong. But I kept having them.

When I turned fourteen my father took a job overseas, and my mother, brother and I moved next door to my mother's parents. My 'feelings' resurfaced, not surprisingly: my dad was hardly ever around and, as a teenager, I was fully in my individuation process. I asked again. The answer was the same. I didn't believe it any more, so I went and asked my grandmother. There, finally, I received an honest answer – I learned that my parents were only together because of us, the children. Their marriage was essentially a sham, and had been for many years. I had been right all along. I became a very angry teenager – particularly angry with my mother, not so much for deceiving me but for negating my feelings, for making me wrong. Bless her, she had meant well. She hadn't known that I would find out the truth, or that I would feel so invalidated. Nevertheless, I raged for many years, and only after exhaustive therapy did I 'get over it'.

Over the years, I have worked with a number of children who have had the same kind of experience, and it is always painful; any invalidation of what we know, no matter how young we are, hurts, because it creates insecurities, lack of confidence and lack of trust, and ultimately impairs the relationship between parent and child. Long-term, it also impairs the child's confidence in their own intuition, the foundation for connection to and trust in their own parent-intuition (or lack of) in later life. To avoid this, congruence is essential.

The first and most important step, and often most difficult, is to be completely honest with yourself about what you're feeling. This is also essential if you are to tune in to your child. If your emotion is not congruent with what you're saying to your child or with your actions, it will interfere – literally, in your brain – with your capacity to fully 'tune in' and connect. Make it a priority to do what you can to amend this and to entrain within yourself.

If your child is 'calling you' on your incongruence – for example asking if something is wrong when there is – but your inclination is to deny it, stop yourself. Instead, you might say something like, 'You're right, I am not feeling really great just now. I think I need to see if I can make myself feel better. Thank you for talking to me about it.' You might also give your child a hug and let them know that their love always feels good. If the issue is more long-term and cannot be corrected by short-term means, you may want to let your child know that this is a private or grown-up problem that needs some time to solve, but you appreciate their concern and their love means a lot to you.

How to be congruent

Once you start to become aware of your own three levels of influence and whether they are congruent, you will find yourself choosing to either 1. align your feelings with what you are saying and doing (i.e. manage your emotions and change the way you feel), or 2. look for a way to express your feelings so you are communicating authentically and congruently. (Your child's age and age-appropriate communication will of course always apply.) An example of incongruence might be: you want to appear calm and in control, taking the positive approach, but you're angry with your spouse. Your options are:

1. Get congruent: Take a five- or ten-minute 'parent time-out', letting everyone know you'll be back in ten; go to a private space, the bathroom or for a quick walk, and take a pen and paper or a small journal. Write down what you are thinking and feeling and where in your body you are holding the tension. Then take a deep breath and, as you exhale, let the tension go. Do that a few times. Focus on something else for a moment, such as a flower or blue sky. Allow yourself to appreciate it and feel the appreciation. You may now have a new perspective on your problem and an idea of how best to address it (as you brain is now working better). At the very least you have now managed your emotions so you are more in line with the calm 'all is well' approach you wanted to take with your children. Go back with an 'I've got this handled' attitude.

2. Express authentically: take a few deep slow breaths and say, as calmly as possible, 'I am feeling a bit annoyed with a

grown-up problem right now, but it has nothing to do with you. I will do something to make myself feel better and sort it out.' If you can, this is a good time to use humour, music and doing something physical to actually make yourself feel better. Put on some dance music and get the children dancing with you or go for a run together. If your child has witnessed a disagreement between you and your partner, let them also witness that you have made up – if you go to another room to resolve your issue, they will know when you return if you have really resolved it! If appropriate, resolve it right there in front of them. Witnessing you resolving conflict is how they will learn to manage and resolve it themselves.

Becoming entrained

A few questions to reflect on:

- Where in nature have you observed entrainment?
- When and where in your life have you personally experienced entrainment?
- When have you experienced your child or children entraining with you?
- When were you last aware of your feelings being congruent with your actions and speech?
- Is your current internal state congruent with your actions or what you are about to say?
- What can you do to be more emotionally coherent and have your children entrain with you?

A perfect example of an adult entraining the children in her care is Mary Poppins. Watch her! She demonstrates a combination of clarity, direction, boundaries, fun and magic – all while her own emotions are practically perfectly managed. I have found the example can be especially helpful because of the fun, humour and playfulness, or 'magic', the character Mary Poppins brings. I shared this with one young mother who was particularly frustrated with her three-year-old on a daily basis. Her little girl was exceptionally fussy about what underwear she wore and every morning, just as the family was getting ready to leave the house, her daughter would want to change her underwear, refusing to leave until she was wearing 'the right pair'. The parents became extremely frustrated at this daily occurrence, as it invariably made them late for work and her older brothers late for school. In these situations, the parents' management of their own internal state was proving to be difficult at best. Referencing Mary Poppins, the mother complained to me that 'it's all right for her, she had magic on her side!'

I suggested she and her daughter created their own magic. For example, as they were dressing, they could 'speak to the underwear' and ask the whole drawer of underpants which was the right one to wear today. The mother could listen as if hearing the underwear speak, and could ask her daughter if she could hear them. Then, they could act as if they had heard a particular pair of pants say it wanted to be worn by the little girl. At first, the mother looked at me as if I were mad, but eventually agreed to try my suggestion.

The very next week she came back to me, smiling broadly. The 'magic' had worked. Her little girl had at first said she wasn't sure she could hear her underwear, but was fascinated with her mother's new ability, and had happily worn the selected underwear without complaint. Increasingly she began to claim she could hear the 'right' underwear too and stopped asking to change again. The humour of the situation had additionally helped both mum and dad to stay calm and centred, and the family now left for school and work each morning in an entrained state (most days).

Chapter 4

Your Personal Parenting Blueprint

'Values are like fingerprints. Nobody's are the same, but you leave 'em over everything you do.' Elvis Presley

A TOOL TO HELP RESIST PARENTING PEER PRESSURE

Whenever we feel insecure or incoherent, whether as parents or individuals, one element will always exacerbate it and that is the opinion of others, especially those we care about.

Whether we experience actual peer pressure or we merely have thoughts and imaginings in our minds, what others think of us can have a debilitating effect on the choices we make. It can also seriously interfere with our intuition and whether we listen to or act on that intuition – on what we feel is right.

We all have one tool that can help us with this, however, one resource that can function like a blueprint for our real authentic selves, for our decisions and the choices we make. It is a tool that can give us clarity, help us define our purpose, and give us effective and valuable guidance for managing all our relationships. It will help us know which 'battles to pick' in those relationships, especially with our children. Some would even say this tool works like a blueprint for our very life's purpose. Whether we are aware of such a blueprint or not, whether we draw on it or not, it will always play a major role in our responses to life's events because it determines in large part *why* we have the stress reactions we have, those stress reactions that are personal, emotional and specific to us.

This tool or blueprint consists of one thing: our very own personal, unique core values. Although we can be largely aware of our core values, we can nevertheless be oblivious to their practical significance. Core values are the answer to the question 'In a world where you could select what your life was to be about, where your life had a purpose that would leave a legacy, what would you choose?'[*] Your core values could be defined as your 'global desired life consequences'.[†]

THE POWER OF CORE VALUES

It has always fascinated me that whenever I ask someone about their core values, I am more or less guaranteed a question in response: 'What are yours?' followed by 'I know I should have thought about my values, but I really haven't given it much thought.' Although core values are the main indicator of what is most important, even vital, to each of us, many if not most people seem to be unaware of their

[*] K. G. Wilson and A. R. Murrell, 'Values Work in Acceptance and Commitment Therapy', in S. C. Hayes, V. M. Follette and M. Linehan (eds), *Mindfulness & Acceptance: Expanding the Cognitive-behavioral Tradition* (Guilford Press, 2004), p. 135.
[†] S. C. Hayes, K. Strosahl and K. G. Wilson, *Acceptance and Commitment Therapy* (Guilford Publications, 1999), p. 206.

values, especially those that are their personal core values (as opposed to those they might find appealing or like to have, or that are foisted upon them by their religious faiths or community). It is unsurprising, therefore, that many of our behaviours and actions are not always in line with our core values, and that this in turn impacts our sense of self and our self-assurance.

When our personal core values are violated – whether we are conscious of those core values or not – it can trigger feelings of discomfort, irritation, upset, stress, anger or occasionally even rage, which can result in complete loss of control of our behaviour. When we *are* conscious of a core value and its significance to us, we become willing to make great, even life or death, sacrifices to defend that value. Our core values determine many of our deeply held beliefs, and what 'feels' right and what 'feels' wrong. Unfortunately, many of us are not drawing on or consciously applying our core values in any other way but reactionary, mainly because we are not consciously aware of what they are. This is a shame because they are, as I say, a tool and a very powerful one at that – especially for parents.

Of course, most parents know that values are important. You may have considered the significance of values in your life and in relationships even before you were a parent. But *knowing* that and consciously *applying* your particular and distinctive core values to your parenting is another thing altogether. Consciously living and parenting according to your core values day to day requires first that you have clearly identified them, independently from the prevailing values of the society and community in which you live, which as universal collective values are likely to be fine, virtuous and aligned to yours, but are nevertheless not necessarily your own subjective, personal core values.

Personal core values are significantly more important because, first of all, they determine your triggers and therefore what naturally creates the most stress for you and for your parenting. Whether you are aware of the origin of those triggers or they appear from your subconscious too fast for you to control, they will drive your emotional reactions. Increasing your awareness of these triggers and their underlying values-based cause can help you set limits in a more proactive and emotionally managed way than you otherwise might, helping you to mindfully 'pick your battles'.

Additionally, and some would say even more importantly, your core values are significant for your children's sense of belonging and their development. Being raised with a considered and clear set of core values builds self-awareness and confidence, resilience and resistance to peer pressure, and helps build a healthy self-image. Shared family core values also build empathy and consideration, and that includes consideration for you, the parent (remember you are not just a source of support and supplies, or a taxi service). Parents have feelings that children need to learn to consider. This is central to them developing skills for friendships, relationships and expressing love in life generally.

As your children grow and individuate from you, even as they select a few core values of their own, the values they have already integrated will become increasingly significant, helping them resist peer pressure and make informed choices in response to the situations to which they are exposed. Neuroscientist and child psychiatrist Daniel Siegel is one of a number of researchers who have studied the impact of values-based parenting on the ability of adolescents to resist peer pressure.

CORE VALUES AND THE ADOLESCENT BRAIN

In his book *Brainstorm: The Power and Purpose of the Teenage Brain*, Siegel references research into the adolescent brain and recent discoveries about the nature of impulse control, risk-taking and addiction changes as the brain develops. The teenage brain – being in the developmental process of seeking, adventuring and finding an identity separate from the person's 'tribe of origin'– is particularly prone to viewing the pros rather than the cons of anything the rest of us might perceive as risky or reckless. As a result, an adolescent is more likely to go out on a limb in search of a thrill, especially if their 'internal conscience' and strength of their values are weaker than the allure of the temptation or the goading of peers.

There is plenty of evidence to show that if someone is going to become addicted to smoking cigarettes or taking drugs, they are most likely to start in the teenage years. Siegel quotes studies done by public health authorities in the United States that found that teenagers were not discouraged from smoking by their parents' rules or dictates, or by health warnings or even by vivid images of horrendous outcomes.* The one approach that made teens stop smoking was

---

* Daniel J. Siegel, *Brainstorm: The Power and Purpose of the Teenage Brain* (Jeremy P. Tarcher, 2013), pp. 80–2.

when they were informed that the cigarette company executives were brainwashing them by glamorising smoking in order to make money. This approach worked because it focused their attention on values such as integrity, honour, honesty and personal strength standing up to exploitation (as well as, I imagine, a youthful defiance to the corporate status quo).

Integrating core-values-based reflections and boundaries can be a powerful tool, giving young people the capacity for impulse control when they most sorely need it. It also tends to build healthy social skills generally and the ability to collaborate. All these positive qualities will be enhanced in any of us, of course, at any age, as we become more aware of and apply our core values in more conscious ways.

IDENTIFYING CORE VALUES

You may be one of the rare parents who has already identified your core values, in which case I suggest you read the rest of this chapter for the possibility that you may discover even more ways to apply them, but also because you may find that your values are more valuable as a tool than you had realised. If, on the other hand, you have not yet ascertained your unique and specific core values, you are in good company.

In my twenty-five years of working with parents, I have yet to meet one parent who has already done this to their own satisfaction. For many, one simple reason may be that the question has just never come up, or that the required self-awareness and self-reflection have not been given enough priority. We are not helped by the ever-increasing amount of distractions, demands and over-stimulation to which we are subjected daily, because this all takes us out of ourselves – our attention gets focused away from our internal experiences onto external stuff that may be mesmerising, and that we may prioritise at that moment, but invariably has little if anything to do with our core values and the way we really want to live our lives.

Living and parenting according to your own core values necessitates being present with yourself as well as having an awareness of what your values are. Identifying those that are uniquely yours begins with recognising that they are in fact key to who you are and determine what makes you feel authentic, and that their violation creates many of the triggers and stress-reactions you experience. In other words, the difference between what creates stress for you and what creates stress for me lies largely in our differences in values and which values we prioritise as core.

Try this:

Take a few moments to reflect on what your unique triggers are, what really pushes your buttons and that you feel righteous about – then explore which value is being violated when you're being triggered. The value violated will very likely be one of your core values. For example, one of my triggers is injustice – especially when it comes to innocence. Whenever I witness it, the anger I feel is not something I want to change; rather, I want to channel it into action, to speak up and do something, however small, to stop the injustice. This indicates several core values – justice, compassion and advocacy. Here are a few examples of common triggers and the corresponding value that may be violated by them.

Trigger	Value
Hypocrisy, corruption, duality	Integrity
Inequality, oppression, wrongdoing	Justice, fairness
Unfaithfulness, betrayal	Loyalty
Moroseness, self-centred grumpiness	Humour
Apathy, indifference	Passion
Greed, meanness	Generosity
Ingratitude, taking things/ people for granted	Appreciation, thankfulness
Contempt, irreverence	Respect
Spitefulness, thoughtlessness	Kindness
Disdain, hostility	Compassion, benevolence
Hate, neglect	Love, care
Lies, deceit, pretence	Honesty
Subordination/dependency	Independence, freedom

Once you have identified your core values – and you may typically find you have somewhere between five and ten – put them aside and consider your child or children: imagine that years in the future they are leaving home and when you go to bed you are able to sleep well because you know they embody five core values. Which would those core values be?

When you have identified the values you hold most dear for your children, those you wish them to embody and live by when they leave your care, try this: write them down. Next to each value, list the behaviours and actions that you associate with that value.

Value	Associated Behaviours & Actions	Social Skills
e.g. *Integrity*	*Mean what you say/say what you mean*	*Follow through on promises*

Having established your core values, it can be helpful to remember that they won't necessarily be imparted to or integrated in your children by osmosis. Exploring ways to integrate them into your lives is a natural next step. One way of ensuring this, which I have used with a great number of families, is to create an 'Our Family Values' chart.

CREATING A FAMILY CORE-VALUES CHART

Gather the family around a table and have paper and colour pencils, crayons or markers ready, and initiate a conversation about values. You may want to use a story to illustrate values, or just explain what core-values are. (Try to keep it to a few sentences, so as not to lecture.) Share the values that are most important to you and why, then ask your children what one of their values might be. Aim to make it a reflective process, encouraging them to share while you listen – try to be open and non-judgemental. Encourage everyone to write down their values and really explore what each one might indicate and entail in practice. Then decide how they overlap and what you have in common. Use a Venn diagram to make it more visual. Add a circle for each member of the family that takes part, and make sure that there is a bit in the middle where all the circles overlap.

In the sections on either side, write your individual core values.
In the centre note down those that you have in common
or that are complementary and clearly compatible.

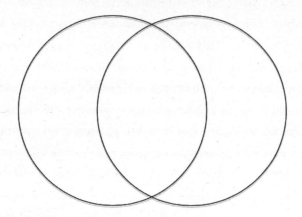

The values in the centre of the Venn diagram are your core family values. Write them on a large piece of paper. Those of you who like to be artistic, decorate the page until it's ready to frame and hang up somewhere clearly visible to everyone. From then on, you can all reference your values whenever it's relevant, and point out a value that may have been violated. You may want to explore the possible natural consequences of going against each family value with your partner and with your children of an appropriate age. Consider it a chance to be proactive and establish boundaries. Talking about and preparing for the outcome of breaching a value with children can be a good teaching opportunity, and a way to develop and deepen understanding – and even possibly reach an agreement – as opposed to creating a power struggle that so often occurs when we try to discipline a child and impose a consequence in the heat of the moment.

When a family values chart has been thoroughly reflected on and created, it will not only become a powerful reference and guidepost for everyone in the family – and for your parenting – but also ensure the integration of those values in your children. In his book, Siegel writes about the importance of instilling a genuine sense of a positive value, so that adolescents develop the capacity for aiming *for* something rather than inhibiting something: 'Instead of trying to shut down an impulse by inhibiting it, adults with adolescents in their lives should focus on a positive factor to promote. Encouraging the reflection on values, is the difference between turning down a compelling impulse and embracing a thoughtful belief and value.'

In my experience, *embracing a thoughtful belief and value* is one direct result of a parent being tuned in – to oneself and to one's children. Becoming familiar with and consciously implementing our core values is actually an enjoyable expression of who we are and the love we have for our children. It can be a most pleasurable experience leading to an invaluable gift for our children, in their tenuous adolescence and beyond. In the next few chapters, I will address what gets in the way of these two keys to being tuned in that we've explored already: why *aren't* we naturally coherent and congruent in our communication with our little ones, and why does parenting from our core values present a challenge for so many of us? After all, these two parenting qualities, integrated and applied, should be a no-brainer.

Chapter 5

Expectations
Those that help and those that hinder

'*Do not ask that your kids live up to your expectations.*
Let your kids be who they are and your expectations
will be in breathless pursuit.' Robert Brault, *Short*
Thoughts for the Long Haul (CreateSpace, 2017)

If you were to make a list of the issues and resulting feelings that get in the way of you being the parent you really want to be and tuned in to what I like to call the 'one-rule' of parenting – using your intuition – you may gain some important insights. I have done so myself and had clients do it over the years, countless times, and there is one insight that comes up for just about everyone: that expectations are an issue. Whether they are conscious or unconscious, initially well-intentioned and positive, or gradually proven to be unrealistic, most expectations parents have of their children will, at the very least, become stress-producing. I want to speak of expectations here – specifically separating those that are helpful from those that are unlikely to be – because they can so easily, even if inadvertently, get in the way of us arriving at the result we really want. Unfortunately, it's all too easy to discover this when damage has already been done.

There are two schools of thought about having specific expectations of our children – in my experience either of them can be spot-on or wholly unhelpful. The issue is in how they are applied and whether they are supportive of the child in question or cause disruption to the child's developmental process. These two types of expectations (or expectancies) are:

a) expecting your child to BE a certain way, with specific qualities, ambitions and beliefs;

b) expecting a child to DO what it takes to accomplish certain goals and achievements, set (whether consciously or unconsciously) by you the parent.

EXPECTATION TO 'BE'

Let's look at who we might expect our child to 'be' first. We all have several very natural expectations of our children when they are born. If they are our biological children, we expect certain physical traits to show up, and their personalities and temperaments to be similar to other family members'. If the child is not our biological offspring, we still tend to expect, or at the very least hope, that this child will live up to our aspirations.

These aspirations or expectations can be entirely unconscious and are often based on our own childhood, sometimes on values we're not communicating effectively, occasionally on a subconscious bias, or on ideas and beliefs we hold that are incongruent with the actual reality of our child's nature. When we become fully conscious of these expectations or the fact that they are not being met, it usually follows a series of disappointments – disappointment in how our child is developing or the character traits they are displaying, or even the choices they are making.

As with many disappointments in other human beings, our expectations of our children can be unrealistic and out of touch with their nature and temperament – with who they are, in their essence. When, as a parent, you hold on to your disappointment, it unfortunately activates your 'emotional brain', diminishing the neural activity necessary for a balanced and tuned-in perspective. The result is compromised clarity of thought, which in turn interferes with your potential for supportive communication that might help your child to blossom in their unique way, however divergent from your desires and expectations that way might be.

EXPECTATIONS AND THE BRAIN'S THREAT SYSTEM

Clarity of thought requires your neo-cortex – that large part of the brain at the top and front, sometimes referred to as the 'Seat of Thought' – to be fully switched on and engaged. This 'thinking brain' strategises, plans, is creative and problem-solves. It also gives us the ability to tune in to our intuition and gain the insight we otherwise would not access – those 'aha' moments or times when we spontaneously think outside the box. And maybe most importantly, it allows us to identify feelings, our own and those of others, and to empathise and connect with others in an empathic way, giving us the ability to see life accurately from our child's perspective.

While it additionally gives us the capacity to have a language for our emotions and to express those feelings in a variety of ways, it does not control our emotional life. That is done by our limbic system (as mentioned in the Introduction), that small but most powerful part of the brain located deep in its lower centre. When messages are filtered through this part of the brain – as they are continuously – the question is repeatedly posed: 'Am I threatened?'* Within the context of what is known and stored by your brain from your specific experiences, the situation is perceived and compared to previous and similar situations. If a rough match is found, the 'Seat of Thought' or 'thinking brain' is effectively bypassed as instructions are sent straight to the physiology (heart, lungs, digestive tract, etc.) to ready it for a response to the perceived threat (the limbic system assumes the threat is physical). This process happens at immense speed and is usually entirely unconscious. Following this, information then goes to the neo-cortex for the appropriate and more conscious, suitable response. 'How can I apply this to my expectations of my child?' you might well ask.

Well, in simplified terms, our brains have just this one system for dealing with threat, so even if our parent-ego feels threatened (or our parental expectations, our self-respect or our parent-pride) when a child is temperamental, uncooperative or uncommunicative, our brain's 'knee-jerk' threat system will be initiated and the 'thinking brain' will be compromised until – and if – we take charge of it. As a parent, when you experience your child's behaviour as a threat of

---

* Joseph LeDoux, *The Emotional Brain* (Simon & Schuster, 1996); Antonio Damasio, *The Feeling of What Happens* (Mariner, 2000).

sorts, whether a threat to your ideals, desires, expectations or even pride, unless you make a conscious choice to take charge of yourself and change that response, it can be a significant contribution to stress-driven reactions that you may later regret.

Your child's threat system

Of course, this doesn't just happen to you. It happens to your child, too. The threat system of your child's brain is equally active, in fact some would say even more so as they have a much less developed cortex – the many centres in their 'thinking brain' are still in development and, depending on their age, some centres not developed at all. For example, at age four, even though a child has begun to recognise signs of emotions and match their own with appropriately learned responses (a stage known as 'learned empathy'), any capacity for genuine empathy that places others before oneself has not yet developed.

If any child feels that they have not lived up or cannot live up to your expectations, their self-image will begin to become deflated. A child's foundation for their sense of self is greatly rooted in their relationship with you, their parent, and your acceptance and love for the person they are becoming, that they are blossoming into. I do not mean to suggest you accept all their behaviour or actions, but rather that you choose to tune into and act from an understanding and acceptance of their personality, temperament, developmental stage and emotional experience. If a child experiences a rejection of the person they feel they are, or they perceive an expectation (from you) for them to be someone they do not feel they are or can live up to, their brain's threat system is going to become active and emotional pain will ensue.

For decades now, scientific discoveries have shown that the areas of the brain responsible for emotional change in response to experience are affected not only by the emotional environment in which a child is raised, but also by repeated experience.[*] This would indicate that the more often a child experiences themselves as 'not good enough' or disappointing you by just being who they are, the more permanent those neural pathways become and the more solidified their belief will be that they are 'just not enough'. As you can no doubt imagine, and maybe even experience yourself, this can be a deeply held belief that is carried through our entire life.

YOUR CHILD IS ONE OF A KIND

When I was an adolescent, I discovered the Gestalt prayer by Frans Perl: 'I am not in this world to live up to your expectations and you are not in this world to live up to mine. You are you and I am I and if by chance we meet, it's beautiful.' I found it on a plaque which I duly bought and which went up on the wall of every home I had from then on until my own daughter was grown. It started off as a validation of what I instinctively knew, in part as a result of not feeling I was good

---

[*] Donald Hebb, *The Organization of Behaviour* (John Wiley & Sons, 1949); C. M. Bishop, *Neural Networks for Pattern Recognition* (Oxford University Press, 1995); E. P. Bauer, J. E. LeDoux and K. Nade, 'Fear Conditioning and LTP in the Lateral Amygdala Are Sensitive to the Same Stimulus Contingencies', *Nature Neuroscience*, vol. 4, no. 7 (2001); Norman Doidge, *The Brain that Changes Itself* (Penguin, 2007).

enough when I was a child, and ended up being a great reminder of that same thing: each child is special, and unique, and enough.

While we all know this theoretically, applying it to a child who has just disappointed you terribly can be tough. It definitely requires you, at that very point, to refocus on the fact that your child is one of a kind and may differ from you in some significant ways and even sometimes annoy you terribly, especially when they are attempting to assert their individuality.

For those moments, I'd like to offer a suggestion that I and hundreds of my clients have found invaluable, using the following metaphor: imagine your life as a garden filled with flowers. See each of your children as special flowers in that garden, and while you yourself might be a rose (and you might naturally expect your children to be roses), what if your daughter is a lily or a daisy? Or your son is an iris or geranium? All the flowers are equally beautiful and have equal value, yet they have differing needs. For example, a rose requires a slightly acidic soil, while none of the other flowers do well in acidic soil. Some flowers require more sun than others, some better drainage. So, whatever *you* need to flourish may not be what your child needs. This may sound simplistic, but it can be helpful to bear in mind exactly *because* it is simple.

A family I once worked with in Hawaii loved the ocean. They would all spend their spare time swimming and surfing in the waves – except for the youngest daughter. She was apprehensive of the ocean at best and would much rather be reading or painting at home. The more her parents or older siblings pushed her to enjoy the ocean, the

more stubbornly she refused. When they finally decided to appreciate her uniqueness, it helped them change their perspectives.
Creative ideas followed and they ended up with a parasol, a small
tent, an easel and a basket full of paints and books accompanying
them to the beach. Their daughter was delighted that she got to do
what she loved on the beach – painting her family playing in the
waves. When the pressure was off, she gradually found the ocean less
and less threatening and increasingly inviting. Eventually, she found
her way into the warm waters.

Try this:

Keep the image of different flowers in mind or hang some flower
pictures up on the kitchen wall to remind you. Use the garden reference to help you step away from the restrictions of expectations and
judgements, and instead take a few deep breaths and allow yourself
to find what you appreciate about your child's innate uniqueness.
Approaching your child from a place of wonder at their blossoming
into a unique being who you are gradually getting to know will make
you better able to discover their true innate strengths and qualities,
and to support them to be more of who they are (rather than having
them struggle to meet your approval).

Try this:

If your child behaves in a way that is unacceptable to you, make sure
you separate their behaviour from who they are. For example, 'You are
disgraceful!' is only going to make them feel small and defensive, and
their brain's threat mechanism will shut down any opening that might
allow them to listen to you. Conversely, 'I understand you are upset,
but I need you to find a more appropriate way to show it. That

behaviour is unacceptable. You can use words to let us know what you're feeling,' will more likely lead you to a next stage of dialogue that can be an opportunity to teach rather that demonising who they are.

Give your child space to calm down and then (and only then) have a chat about why they may have behaved in the way you found unacceptable. It is important here that you validate their feelings and show some empathy before talking about why the behaviour was not acceptable. You may then want to refer to your agreed-upon values or ask your child how they could have done things differently. Once there is an agreed-upon re-framing of the behaviour, ask them to agree to doing it that way next time they feel whatever they felt.

EXPECTATION TO 'DO' AND PERFORM

The other expectation that can go awry and get in the way – or conversely, if done right, can actually be helpful – is the parental expectancy related to performance and effort. The obvious flag in terms of it going awry is your own unmet expectations of yourself, and attempting to live vicariously through your children's achievement. If this resonates even slightly with you, I suggest you stop reading, take a walk and maybe give yourself some space to write your thoughts and feelings in a journal. If you conclude that there is a chance your parenting in this area may be causing stress to your child, use this chapter to help you gain insights into what may be a healthier more helpful perspective for all.

Parental expectations that relate to 'doing' and to performance often originate from the expectations of family, friends, community and even neighbours. The desire to be accepted by a particular community, or to not stand out from the crowd, initiates the brain's same 'threat system' and prevents parents from listening to and following their own intuition. When parents also have a need to compete with other parents, for their child to be admired and praised for their achievements, the pressure and accelerated stress levels that follow can be damaging to the child, the parent and the parent–child relationship.

Conversely, expectations that emphasise the child's innate interest and the *process* of learning, as well as the goal, will create a much healthier and pressure-free approach. A focus that helps the child to expand their curiosity, and develop the skills of integrating and applying the relevance of their acquired knowledge to achieving accomplishments, will also help develop resilience and the capacity to self-motivate, to handle challenges and to bounce back from disappointments. For parents, managing and letting go of the pressure and stress caused by trying to live up to others' expectations allows the brain to 'switch on' and think clearly. This management of the brain's threat system is necessary for any parent to be able to fully tune in to their child and what is most appropriate for them, and ultimately to act on that intuition, encouraging growth rather than pushing a specific agenda or expectation.

A GROWTH MINDSET VERSUS A FIXED MINDSET

A popular saying in the 1960s, 'Becoming is better than being', expressed the idea that growth was more desirable than a permanent state. It is a notion whose time has come again – this time around not so much as an ideology but as a result of research.*

As a young (and very average) student ballet dancer, I was fleetingly encouraged by a claim I read somewhere that to be successful required 2 per cent talent and 98 per cent hard work. Unfortunately, my teachers hadn't read the same article and my efforts seemed to go unnoticed, with almost all attention from my teachers being given to those who showed more obvious talent. I felt increasingly discouraged and timid, gradually withdrawing from situations where my lack of self-confidence might be reinforced. The success I sought seemed to elude me and I gave up on a ballet career. Two different careers later, as a dance teacher, I discovered that I had been raised with a not-so-helpful 'fixed' mindset: a consequence of natural talent and abilities being praised and rewarded, while mistakes and efforts that fall short are indicators of lack of ability and to be discouraged or avoided. Conversely, a 'growth' mindset – viewing faults and failure as opportunities for growth – is a mindset that, I discovered, not only gradually reveals untapped abilities but also can open doors to previously unimagined possibilities.

The terms 'growth mindset' and 'fixed mindset' were coined by one of the leading researchers in the field, Professor Carol Dweck at Stanford University, who is also often credited with popularising the

* Ellen Leggett, 'Children's Entity and Incremental Theories of Intelligence', paper presented to the Eastern Psychological Association, Boston (1985); C. S. Dweck and E. L. Leggett, 'A Social-cognitive Approach to Motivation and Personality', *Psychological Review*, vol. 95, no. 2 (1988).

'Becoming is better than being' quote.* Her research has attracted increasing attention among educators and mental health professionals because her findings show that, rather than focusing on intelligence and innate achievement, it is far more important to reward effort, creative strategies and perseverance.

This growth mindset is all about 'becoming'. It views the process, the effort, the 'journey', the growth itself as having more value than 'being' in the accomplished state. Although we are all inclined to praise intelligence and ability in both ourselves and our children, research shows that excessive praise actually creates a 'fixed mindset', resulting in fragile people without the resilience needed to effectively tackle adversity or persevere in the face of difficulty. With such a mindset, when we feel rejected or disappointed, we immediately think 'I'm not likeable. I'm not approved of – I'm not a good enough person', feeling guilt or shame for having done something negative or failing to achieve a goal. With a growth mindset, however, we think, 'I am not happy with what I did. It may be inconsistent with my values. How can I better understand it? What can I learn from it? How can I make up for it and improve in the future?'

Dweck is often asked to compare her findings with the ever-popular cognitive behavioural therapy (CBT), and her response is particularly interesting: 'CBT often says "Don't think you're not a smart person because you didn't get an A. Look at all the other A's you got – you're a smart person." But in the mindset framework, we're saying

* Carol S. Dweck, *Mindset: The New Psychology of Success* (Random House, 2006).

"Get out of the smart-person framework entirely. Stop thinking about the good or bad measures but rather think of yourself as a work in progress." CBT asks you to find evidence to challenge the argument, and we're saying it's the wrong argument.'

I find this particularly interesting because it validates and supports my experience and work developing Applied Emotional Mastery® – where the focus is on feeling and using the management of emotions to help better understand, learn from and continuously improve – whether it's in relationships, parenting, managing others or opening our own mind up to more possibilities; in other words, to develop a growth mindset.

MINDING YOUR PRAISE

So, while talent, natural abilities, interests and strengths can be important guiding lights for the direction a child takes, evidence clearly shows that it is the growth mindset that ultimately creates resilience and achieves success. (Had I had such a mindset as a young dancer, who knows, age aside I might still be prancing around 'en pointe'!) Encouragement and praise for effort are key to developing this growth mindset, so when you are tempted to praise accomplishments, comments such as 'I'm so proud of you for getting an A in English!' could imply that you are not proud of the C in Science even though this may have taken a much greater effort. If this type of praise is frequent, it can eventually leave your child merely pursuing what they naturally find easy, avoiding attempting anything new or uncomfortable and thereby not developing their capacity to challenge themselves, to learn new things and stretch their ability.

To your child, your parental pride is tied up with the love and approval they desperately need from you. If it is primarily expressed through a focus on achievement, it can, to your child, feel like conditional love, which may result in a host of unintended problems in the teenage years and beyond.

THE BRAIN'S INTEGRATION PROCESS

To develop your child's 'growth mindset', it can help to be aware of the brain's learning process. The parts of the brain structure directly involved in learning and the growth mindset are all located in the cerebral cortex, the large top part of the brain.* Simply put, they include sensing, integrating and action (or motor). Your *senses* experience something (you hear, see, feel, smell or taste something). Your brain identifies it and decides what it is (with whatever references you have that can give context to the experience); what you should do about it (your recognition and past experiences of dealing with anything similar); and when and where you should do it; all this is referred to as *integration*. Finally, signals are sent to the appropriate body parts and the *action* (motor) is carried out. This process happens at lightning speed, many thousands of times during the day.

As we've seen, however, the learning process can be hijacked by the limbic system if the amygdala considers the experience as in any way threatening. When this happens the motor centre is activated by

---

* James E. Zull, *The Art of Changing the Brain* (Stylus, 2002); James E. Zull, 'The Art of Changing the Brain', *Educational Leadership*, vol. 62, no. 1 (2004).

'instructions' effectively sent straight from the amygdala – bypassing the integration centres, and 'defence' action occurs at once. In a child, this could look like distraction, attention difficulties, withdrawal or blatant refusal to learn. There are many degrees of this but, in simple terms, for anyone to learn and integrate their learning, they must feel safe and not have the limbic system active. If it is active, the learning will likely merely reflect their reaction to the perceived threat.

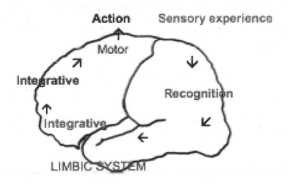

Once we ensure that the learner feels safe, learning that 'sticks' requires recognition, reflection and observation, the development of ideas and concepts, and active testing of those ideas and your perceptions of them. As your child's parent, you can facilitate this by setting aside your own expectations and 'meeting' your child where that child is, emotionally and mentally.

MEETING YOUR CHILDREN WHERE THEY ARE

If your child has no reference frame or context within which to place their experience or what they are learning, they cannot integrate the learning; it 'bounces back out'. Ask yourself:

Does your child fully understand the communication? How can you help your child recognise and fully comprehend the message?

If your child feels threatened in any way, the limbic system is activated, the 'thinking brain' is surpassed and the only integration that takes place is the learning about whatever they feel threatened by (fight or flight). As we now know, this can equally be an imagined or perceived threat that results in a 'short circuit' of potential learning.

What is your child's emotional state? Is it defensive?

First establish if the feeling is warranted, i.e. if your child is indeed being threatened in the learning environment. If so, this should be addressed with the adult in question. Conversely, if you establish that the threat is perceived (for instance, in a bad dream or because of a possible failure that your child anticipates will manifest itself), how can you effectively help calm and centre your child, 'switching on' their 'thinking brain'?

If positive emotions (i.e. curiosity or interest) are not engaged in the learning process, the parts of the brain involved in the integrative process will not be engaged and therefore less or often no learning or integration will take place. This may be due to your child's mindset – they may have been 'over-praised' excessively for their natural ability, or they could have become insecure and lost confidence and motivation when under too much pressure to perform. Either way:

What can you do to engage your child, putting them in a more positive, curious and self-motivated state? You may want to examine how you've been communicating.

If you have been over-praising, consider switching your encouragement from saying 'Good job!' all the time to instead challenging your child somewhat, e.g. 'I can see you're working hard at that picture. I'm so proud of you! What more can you do?' This will ultimately encourage effort and help create a growth mindset. In addition, it will help you as a parent to determine more realistic expectations of your child's abilities. Your child needs to be able to assess their strengths and weaknesses themselves. They need to develop the ability to monitor and refine their own performance. You can help your child by giving clear and realistic encouragement, supportive but simultaneously authentic.

If, on the other hand, you determine your child has been pushed too hard, you may alter your language to encourage your child to slow down a tad, and find ways to view the process itself as motivating. You can contribute to this by setting an example. For instance, if your child is in the kitchen with you as you're about to cook, you may say; 'This recipe is quite complicated. Maybe I'll start by sorting out and measuring the ingredients first.' Encourage your child to ask questions and give opinions.

Try this:

When you have a quiet ten minutes, take a pen and paper and write down any disappointment you might have about how your child is developing or the choices your child is making.

One of the quickest ways to release disappointment from un-met expectations is to give your attention instead to 'what is' and appreciate qualities that make your child uniquely who they are. List some things you can appreciate in your child – what is innately in the child you love.

Make a pact with yourself to focus on at least three of the things from your list, each and every morning. Write down what they are and how/when you will remember to do this, and bring them to mind when your child is challenging you.

Chapter 6

Tuning In
The ultimate intuitive parenting tool

'*Between stimulus and response there is a space. In that space is
our power to choose our response. In our response lies our growth
and our freedom.*' Attributed to Viktor E. Frankl (1940s)

One of my clients, a dad I'll call Blake, told me excitedly one day
about an interaction between him and his daughter that, as he put it,
'blew him away'. He and his partner had taken their three children to
a funfair. The two older children, both boys, wanted to go on all the
big rides, but his five-year old daughter Kate (not her real name) just
wanted to go on the smallest roller-coaster. Being that small, she
needed an adult to accompany her, so Blake said he'd take her. Little
did he know that the longest queue in the whole funfair was for that
roller-coaster, and (not being English) he detested queuing up. But
having committed to going with her, he grudgingly took Kate to join
the queue.

After a while, he began to get impatient and he tried to persuade Kate
that the roller-coaster really was no big deal, but she was adamant.
Then he tried to tempt her with other rides and things he knew she
liked, and finally he became so irritated he offered her a bribe; if they
went on another ride instead, he would give her an extra ice-cream.

As he said it, he told me, he felt bad. But before he could think of a way to backtrack, Kate placed her hands on her hips, turned her little face up to him and said crossly, 'Dad, I have waited my whole life to go on a roller-coaster, I'm not going to give it up now!'

When he recounted the episode to me he added, 'Can you imagine her speaking to me as if this was of earth-shattering importance?! Her whole life indeed! I mean, she's barely five!' He had first stared at her incredulously. Then he stifled a laugh and suddenly it struck him just how very much he loved his little girl. His feelings shifted from annoyance and almost anger to humour, laughter and love. And then he said, 'After that, I could have stood in that queue with her *all day* and I wouldn't have cared!' He continued, 'It was just so incredible to realise that when I let my emotions get out of control, I lose touch with what's actually important and with how I really want to parent!'

RECOGNISE: EMOTIONAL AWARENESS

Blake's increased self-awareness is the most significant aspect of this story, because without it he would not have been likely to truly appreciate the significance of his emotions and the impact they had on his perspective. It is said that 'awareness is everything' – I would posit that without it, no personal, parental or professional growth can effectively happen – and at the core of self-awareness is our emotions.

Emotional self-awareness (and I apologise if I am stating the obvious here) means being able to identify and monitor our emotions as they shift. This is a critical factor in understanding the self and being able to develop confidence in one's ability to make personal and parental choices regarding anything significant. A key to such emotional awareness is the understanding that emotions and feelings can actually be viewed as two separate things; we all have emotions, but how are they different from feelings?*

If we consider an emotion as energy moving through the body (energy in motion: e-motion) – a shift in energy patterns that prepares the internal state for action – then, for example, sweaty palms and 'butterflies' in the stomach would indicate an emotion of anxiety, preparing us to act with caution. When we have a subjective awareness of that emotion, it becomes a feeling – in this case the awareness that 'I am feeling anxious – I am nervous.' If someone is unable to identify their emotions and to 'feel their feelings', it follows that they will be unable to appropriately express those feelings, or self-regulate. Any decisions they then make will emerge from a less than optimally functioning brain.

ARE GIRLS AND BOYS EMOTIONALLY DIFFERENT?

The general stereotypical thinking is that females can more easily identify and talk about feelings than males, and although some would like to dispute this, there is a large and meaningful amount of brain

* Antonio Damasio, *The Feeling of What Happens* (Harcourt, 1999); Antonio Damasio, *Looking for Spinoza: Joy, Sorrow and the Feeling Brain* (Harcourt, 2003).

research that validates it.* However, many girls and women tend to stifle certain specific feelings, most notably those that might be interpreted as aggressive. In most cases, girls and women are reluctant to express emotions such as anger, outrage or fury for cultural and societal reasons. Boys and men, on the other hand, are commonly more likely to express their feelings *through* anger, this being one of the only feelings that is acceptable for males to express in many cultures, and they are often unaware of the many other emotions that have built up to culminate in their anger.

Although I recognise that this is somewhat of a generalisation and there are of course a number of exceptions, cultural upbringing and environments do play a huge role in how we relate to and through emotions. Inevitably, whatever the gender, societal or cultural issues, I believe it is equally critical for both genders in all cultures to be supported, in whatever way is appropriate for them, to improve their emotional self-awareness, because such awareness is where emotional intelligence, maturity and any mastery begins, all key ingredients in realising the very potential we have as individual human beings and as parents.

Yet being emotionally aware is not the norm for most people in our society; not in the way we raise our children, nor in the way we generally interact with each other. When we observe or experience an emotion that is not to our liking or that is uncomfortable,

---

* Diane F. Halpern, *Sex Differences in Cognitive Abilities* (fourth edition, Psychology Press, 2012); Larry Cahill, 'An Issue Whose Time Has Come: Sex/Gender Influences on Nervous System Function', *Journal of Neuroscience Research*, vol. 95, nos 1–2 (2017).

disruptive or disturbing in some way, the norm is to try to control it or modify it through addressing *the result* of the emotion; the behaviour. Addressing an emotional experience through behavioural strategies or through the 'logical' thinking or reasoning process, whether it be in parenting, relationships, teaching environments, businesses or elsewhere, is unlikely to have a lasting effect because emotions are considerably more powerful than thinking,[*] and behaviour is a result of both.

If any cognitive logical strategy *does* work, it is because we inadvertently have struck a chord within that particular individual that affects them emotionally. Unless we know the individual very well and can solicit the emotion that will initiate a shift, it is doubtful that a cognitive, logical approach will be anything more than a hit-and-miss process, a short-term solution and not the most effective way of implementing any sustainable emotional shift.

Emotions are physical

Given this fact, it is clear that for cognitive approaches to work, we must first address the actual emotions, our feeling state, to become attentive to how each differing emotion manifests as a state of being in the body.[†] Because emotions are in essence physiological energy, managing them typically requires a physiological awareness – knowing *where* in our bodies we are impacted by

[*] Gerald L. Clore, *Psychology and the Rationality of Emotion* (NCBI, 2017); David D. Franks, 'The Neuroscience of Emotions', *Handbook of the Sociology of Emotions* (Springer, 2006).
[†] Joseph LeDoux, *The Emotional Brain* (Simon & Schuster, 1996).

stress-producing emotions, and where we hold those emotions. It is important here to define what I mean by stress, and differentiate between distress, from the Latin *dis* = bad (as in dissonance), and eustress, from the Greek *eu* = good (as first defined and coined by Dr Hans Selye, the 'father' of stress research, in 1936).* After almost three-quarters of a century of research, it is now very well documented that it is the impact of *distress* that causes damage to our health, and it is this distress I refer to when I use the term stress. The current high increase in our culture of stress-related illness and disease demonstrates the excessive strain most of us place on our bodies as we repeatedly require them to adapt to our emotionally negative reactions, way beyond anything they are designed to do.

EMOTIONS AND STRESS

Wherever in our body we experience *any* strain, illness or tension, indicates the part (or parts) of the body that 'hold' the stress resulting from an unpleasant or negative emotion. One of my teachers at the Institute of Stress-Management used the metaphor of the old-fashioned computer games (I admit this was some time ago): imagine stress being like the Pac-man, searching through our bodies for the weakest place to attach itself to – and when that place is found, to latch onto it and break it down even further! In order to manage our stress-producing emotions, we need to identify those 'weakest places', and pay attention to where in our body we are registering or 'holding'

---

* Hans Selye, *The Stress of Life* (McGraw-Hill, 1956; revised 1978). This is considered by many to be the defining book on stress.

them. Once identified, our stress-producing emotion can be appropriately released – the first step in emotional management, taking charge of that 'space between stimulus and response' (so eloquently described in the quote attributed to Viktor Frankl at the beginning of this chapter).

Try this:

To remind yourself to adopt a new habit, it can be helpful, for example, to tie a piece of string around one of your wrists; it will work best if you choose the wrist on which you don't usually wear anything such as a bracelet or watch. Alternatively, change how you wear any jewellery or, if you wear a watch, wear it on the other wrist. The purpose is to increase your awareness of your body and help you to focus your attention to your body whenever you feel a strong emotion: mentally scan your body and try to find where you are registering the emotion, where your body is tensing. Name your emotion to yourself, and then try to let the tension go.

A small notebook will be an additional help if you can carry one with you and note what you have found: each specific feeling and where in your body you felt it.

Try this:

The following process allows each family member to get in touch with and express their feelings to one another, in a non-verbal way. It can help all ages (from toddlers and up) to identify feelings and express them without fear of confrontation. It can also help us develop awareness and sensitivity to those with whom we live.

Have each family member create a full-body portrait of themselves. It could be a photo or a drawing, painting or a combination, preferably on an A4-size page.

If you can, do this as a family event around a table together.

Give each family member one pad of Post-its, and make sure everyone has a pen or pencil. Place the 'Find the Feeling Word List' (from the back of this book) on the table so that all the family members can see it, and have everyone proceed as follows:

Choose ten or more feeling words that you identify with the most, and write each feeling word on one Post-it page. If your child has not yet learned to write, help them draw faces or create an emoji for each feeling.

As each feeling word is written, stick that Post-it page onto the edge of your individual portrait.

Hang your 'Find the Feeling' portrait on your bedroom door, the wall of the kitchen or somewhere easily visible to all family members.

Each morning (or when something specific happens that may change the way you feel), take the Post-it that most accurately describes the way you feel and stick it onto your portrait, wherever on your body you feel the feeling.

That's it. No words need be spoken – just an awareness that is felt and expressed.

As you pass the children's or other family member's portraits, stop for a moment to check how they are feeling. Even if you do nothing about it, your awareness of your own feelings and of everyone else's feelings will increase your chances of mutual understanding, tolerance, compassion and appreciation, of yourself and each other!

RELEASE: EMOTIONAL MANAGEMENT 101

Once we are aware of having an emotion that is not working for us, the next step is beginning to manage it. Many people think of emotional management as being the same as emotional control. However, *control* – although often a seemingly outward result – is not necessarily a healthy or even effective way to manage emotions. Emotional management requires the ability to distinguish healthy from unhealthy emotions, emotions that work for us from emotions that don't. It also requires enough understanding of our emotions to know how to appropriately self-soothe and express our feelings to others so they are accurately understood. Ultimately, it means making the decision to deal with emotions that are unhealthy or do not work for us and to apply the necessary skills to regulate those emotions so that they do.

In the process of self-regulating, it is vital to acknowledge that every emotion serves a purpose and as such needs to be recognised and validated. Most negative or unpleasant emotions give us information. For example, repeated anger towards the same injustice might indicate that you need to find a more effective way to stand up for yourself; or deep sadness after a loss signals a grief process, something you need to allow yourself time to move through. Other uncomfortable emotions may be an expression of our 'inner child' and, just like any child wanting attention, will need to be 'acknowledged' in order to allow us to take our next step. Numerous emotions are stress-producing to the point where they have to be released before they can be regulated – an oft-neglected aspect of emotional regulation and one that, to my mind, needs more attention. We *all* need to find appropriate ways to release the stress and tension created by our emotions.

RELEASING STRESS-PRODUCING EMOTIONS

What does it mean to release stress-producing emotions appropriately? When we acknowledge the biological fact that our bodies are designed to perform a physical activity in response to stress, we can easily recognise that in response to the feeling of fear, we experience the urge to run; in response to the feeling of anger, most respond with an urge to lash out, and so on. If we don't respond with physical exertion of any kind, the stress hormones released into the bloodstream during a stress reaction become toxic to the body and accompanying muscular tension can become permanent. Therefore, following a stress reaction, the best release must be physical.

Of course, it is not always appropriate to get up and go for a run in the middle of a stressful meeting, or to get out of the car and punch the driver who cut in front of us, much as we might like to. What *is* appropriate is to take responsibility for our own stress reaction, acknowledge that it is in fact our own personal stress response, an emotion that is being created by our brain, and find a way to release it that won't cause further stress, to others or to ourselves. Here are some suggestions for appropriate ways to release stress and tension produced by our emotions:

1. Clench your fists hard and fast, then splay out the fingers with a slight shake as if shaking off water. Do this two or three times, imagining that you're shaking off your tension each time you shake your hands. Follow this with two or three deep breaths, consciously slowing down your exhalations.

2. If you can (for instance, if you are alone in the car), let your tension out in a yell, followed by three slow breaths, focusing your attention in your heart and chest area or placing a hand there. Alternatively, scream into a pillow or let out a long silent scream – again always followed by the three deep breaths, slowing down the exhale.

3. If you can excuse yourself to go to the bathroom, lock yourself in the bathroom with a pen for just a couple of minutes (about as long as it takes you to relieve yourself!). Write out all your feelings, no matter how negative or bizarre, on toilet paper. When you feel complete, drop the toilet paper into the toilet bowl and flush. Watch your words on the toilet paper flush away and 'see' your tension disappearing with it. Then place a hand lightly on your chest and breathe slowly three times.

4. If you can go for a quick walk or run, again imagining 'walking off' or 'running off' your tension. It also helps to slow down your breathing before returning to the situation. Note: If you are with your children or partner, it is important here that you tell them you're coming back and when, before you leave.

5. Other physical tension releases include punching a punching bag, pillow or mattress, stomping or jumping up and down a few times, all followed by the three slow breaths, all of which work well for children.

6. If you are with your children and jointly experiencing tension, frustration or any kind of stress reaction, you may consider a family tantrum. Jump up and down together, shout and scream if you want, and lie down and pound the floor with your fists. This often ends in fits of laughter with the dual effect of dissolving the negative mood and releasing everyone's stress!

You may have other ideas as well! Regardless of what method you use, the earlier you address your stress-making emotions, the better. Immediately, as soon as you become aware, letting go of the tension (appropriately, of course) starts to create that space 'between stimulus and response' that gets you tuned in to your intuition.

Reframe: Emotional mastery and parent intuition

At this point, you have acknowledged your emotion and released the associated stress-making tension, even if it's just with a long exhale, and the decision to now change what you feel can begin with a simple statement or question. If you feel you're calming down already, you may say to yourself, 'This is an emotion my brain is creating. It is not who I am.' You may find the remnants of the emotion dissipate as you slow your breathing.

If, however, the emotion is still strong and consuming you, look at your feet and ask yourself, 'Am I threatened? Am I in danger?' If the answer is 'Yes!' you need to tell your feet to get you out of there! If not, this question may help you to see yourself from the outside (as if you're watching a friend in the same situation) and allow you to shift to a calmer state.

Once your breathing has slowed and you are calmer, you can decide to change the way you feel – to place your thoughts on hold for a moment and 'switch on' that thinking part of your brain that will allow your more insightful, creative, problem-solving, tuned-in capacities to take over.

Either place the tips of your fingers lightly on your chest or just take your internal focus down to the centre of your chest and heart area. Try to sense your heart in the centre of your breathing, and think of something that makes you want to smile – something simple like a scene in nature, a pet or anything you can appreciate (just being alive can work well!) – and allow yourself to re-experience the feeling. Notice where in your body you feel it, and notice any sensation in your chest, specifically your heart area. Allow yourself to smile, also on the inside. Buddhists call this the Inner Smile, and it works wonders for regulating your brain and all the electrical signals in your body, bringing you back into balance and into that 'tuned-in' state.[*]

* Rollin McCraty, 'Heart–Brain Neurodynamics: The Making of Emotions', *Issues of the Heart: The Neuropsychotherapist*, special issue (2015).

When you feel the shift fully integrated (and this will happen faster the more often you use the process), tune in to your own innermost knowing – that intuitive, wise voice inside you. This is the state you are in when your brain is functioning at its highest capacity;[*] as a parent, it is the state you are in when you are most in tune with your child and with the very best way to parent that child. This state will allow deeper insights to come to you, with an often better view about how to handle the original issue.

THE THREE R'S OF TUNING IN

In summary, the three R's of managing emotions – the key to accessing your intuition at will – are: Recognise (self-awareness), Release (let the stress and tension go, physically) and Reframe (change your feeling) so you can fully 'tune in' to your own wisdom and to your child. It is the ultimate mastery of emotions.

Tuning into your child, and helping your child to tune into themselves, is the essence of intuitive parenting. I'll be exploring it further in the next chapter, but as you have read this far into the book, you may want to take a moment to pause and acknowledge your own willingness to grow. Growth as a parent doesn't just happen automatically. Many parents merely default to raising their children the way they themselves were raised and, if it doesn't feel right, become stuck in justifying their way. Others feel overwhelmed – as mentioned in the Introduction – by too much information and become slaves to

---

[*] Rick Hanson, *Hardwiring Happiness* (Rider, 2013); Daniel J. Siegel, *Mindsight: The New Science of Personal Transformation* (Oneworld, 2010).

parenting blogs and googling for answers. Most of us have been in one or the other position. But by choosing to take the path of self-examination and growth, we ourselves develop a growth mindset, and we strengthen our resilience as well as our own connection to what is right for our parenting and most especially for our child. This 'road less travelled' is not necessarily easy. It is reliant on a desire or intention that is strong enough for action, and if you've come this far in this book, chances are you have already done some soul-searching, grown from your struggles and become a little more secure in your sense of self as a parent, more confident in your ability to 'tune in' to your parent intuition. Celebrate it!

Celebrate is what I suggested my client Blake do when he concluded his story: 'Of course, it took almost another hour before we got through the queue and actually got to go on this roller-coaster and I did start to get antsy a couple of times. But each time I did, I looked down at Kate and remembered how much I love my little girl. That prompted me to slow down my breathing and focus on the warm sensation of love in my chest. I could virtually feel my heartbeats calming down and my brain clearing as I breathed. My hyper feelings of impatience literally dissipated and my thinking completely shifted. Amazing stuff! You know, it may not always be easy but it is so, so simple!' Enough said.

Chapter 7

Empowering Your Child
Could you be over-parenting?

> 'In the real world, life is filled with risks – financial, physical,
> emotional, social – and reasonable risks are essential for children's
> healthy development.' Joe Frost, safety crusader, quoted in
> Hanna Rosin, 'The Over-protected Kid', *Atlantic* (April 2014)

Giving your child space, stepping back and loosening the reins is possibly one of the hardest things for a parent to do. As your relationship with your child changes – which it will – you may find yourself worrying about whether you have maximised your child's happiness and chance for success. You may think of what else you can do, how you can protect your child from all the dangers 'out there' and what you can say or give them that will make their life better. Don't. It invariably gets in the way of that most important element of intuitive parenting – being tuned in to that particular, individual and unique child.

Over-parenting

As I touched on in Chapter 2, there is now ample evidence to support the notion that parents can be too involved with their children.[*]

---

[*] Angel L. Harris and Keith Robinson, *The Broken Compass* (Harvard University Press, 2014); Robert Brooks, *Raising Resilient Children* (McGraw-Hill Education, 2002).

Regardless of how loving and caring a parent is, there is a possibility that parental concern and enthusiasm can become meddling, that swooping in to help can disrupt a child's natural learning process, and that parental caring can easily result in 'over-care' – when caring creates stress – and over-parenting. This is when a parent becomes so engaged in planning and running all the child's activities that the youngster does not get enough unsupervised time to play, to be spontaneous, to be bored and daydream, to explore their own internal landscape and develop their own identity separate from that of their parents.

Well-meaning but overinvolved parents can become intrusive, stifling the very development they want to see blossom. For example, if we review our child's homework every single night (and occasionally even finish it for them),[*] or find ourselves competitively cheering opposite other parents at every basketball game, we are at risk of overstepping that line from supportive to intrusive. Psychologist and author of the book *The Price of Privilege*, Madeline Levine, writes 'Intrusion and support are two fundamentally different processes: support is about the needs of the child, intrusion is about the needs of the parent.'[†] No matter how much we love them, if we as parents are identifying too closely with our children and looking to them and their achievements as indicators of our own self-value, we are going to create problems, both for ourselves and for them.

[*]   Erin A. Maloney, Gerardo Ramirez and Elizabeth A. Gunderson, 'Intergenerational Effects of Parents' Math Anxiety on Children's Math Achievement', *Psychological Science*, vol. 26, no. 9 (2015).
[†]   Madeline Levine, *The Price of Privilege* (HarperCollins, 2006).

For parents, over-involvement and over-parenting make it all the more difficult to let go. For the children, it will often leave them feeling more anxious and insecure than, as intended, feeling protected. Most unfortunately, this can lead to them lacking the skills to function independently or to be self-reliant. This develops little by little, and is often not about what a parent says to their child as much as the message the child gets from the parent's actions. A child can easily perceive a parent's intervention or constant presence as giving them the message, 'I don't think you're competent to deal with this alone. I don't think I can trust your ability to succeed by yourself.'

BUILDING SELF-RELIANCE

There is only one way for children – or indeed anyone – to cultivate their abilities, meet their challenges, overcome their difficulties and feel good about their accomplishments, and that is to go through the experience themselves. In order to have a healthy self-image, fulfilling the need to be an accomplished person is a fundamental requirement for all of us. As toddlers, we begin proclaiming our ability to do things ourselves as soon as we can talk. Adolescents and young adults are notorious for expressing their need for independence and the desire to demonstrate that they are capable.

As a parent, if you find it difficult to step back and allow your child more space, remember when they were learning to walk: did you hold onto them permanently as they were taking those first few steps to save them from repeatedly falling over? Probably not. Every child has to learn to walk by falling over a multitude of times. If you are able to evoke your intuitive wisdom and stay tuned in, you will approach all your parenting from the same perspective as you had when your child was learning to walk, and inevitably you will start to see your child's schedule as a part of a bigger picture to support them to develop their authentic self, without having to always please you or meet adults' often unrealistic hopes and expectancies.

Anthropologist Jean Liedloff, in her book *The Continuum Concept*, recounts her experiences living with the Yequana Indians in South America.* The Yequana attitude to childhood, and indeed human nature in general, is that we are innately capable beings: 'A child's curiosity and desire to do things himself are the definition of his capacity to learn, and nothing can heighten the full spectrum of his capacities beyond its inbuilt limits . . . The object of a child's activities, after all, is the development of self-reliance.'

The desire to be self-reliant and proficient never diminishes; it is an ongoing part of human nature and driven by our basic need for advancement. To meet this need in our children means ensuring their environment empowers them to regularly experience becoming capable of fixing a problem if they have one.

OVER-SCHEDULING

Along with well-meant over-parenting often comes over-scheduling. The past few decades have seen a significant increase in parents scheduling children to pursue a variety of enrichment activities, skills and abilities. After-school tutoring is followed by tennis or

* Jean Liedloff, *The Continuum Concept* (Adlibris, 1975).

squash or another sport, and time for dinner is a tiny window before homework and bed. The next day may be the same; after school an extra French class followed by piano lessons and (again) dinner on the run before homework and falling into bed. The hope is that the child will become well-rounded with all the enrichment, knowledge and range of skills to succeed in life. For extra-curricular activities to truly benefit the child, however, there needs to be a balance with enough free time, adequate sleep, plenty of quality family time (i.e. face-to-face, without devices) and 'just hanging out with no goal' time with parents.*

When time spent together is all about a child's achievement, the child will begin to see their self-worth linked to how they perform – which is when it backfires. Conversely, 'just hanging out with no goal in mind' shows your child that you love them without needing any achievement or activity, and when children feel unconditionally loved in that way, they feel safe and are more likely to become resilient adults. According to Polly Young-Eisendrath, a clinical psychologist and author of *The Self-esteem Trap*, before adolescence, when self-awareness and consciousness really develop, activities risk distracting children from their natural development: 'Prior to that [age], children really need that time to lie around, play more freely, and be side by side with their parents in the same room, being alone together.'†

---

* Alvin Rosenfeld and Nicole Wise, *The Over-scheduled Child: Avoiding the Hyper Parenting Trap* (St Martin's Griffin, 2001).
† Polly Young-Eisendrath, *The Self-esteem Trap* (Little, Brown, 2009).

I am not suggesting that your child shouldn't have any extra-curricular activities, but rather that you use your well-managed parent intuition to find a considered and well thought-through approach, with choices that are in your child's fields of interest and truly are enriching their particular wellbeing needs (rather than necessarily making you proud or meeting your expectations). Create a schedule that gives plenty of time for free, unsupervised outdoor play, with a balanced approach that allows for your child to be doing activities they really enjoy, in some cases with you there and in other cases on their own.

Try this:

1. In a quiet moment, stand in front of a mirror and ask yourself if your child's schedule is balanced or if it is designed (in whole or in part) to meet your own aspirations. Be honest with yourself – which for most of us is easier when we're face-to-face with ourselves, no matter how crazy it seems.

2. Ask your child if they want you at the game or activity. Then respect their wishes.

3. Notice your child's mood when you drop them off and pick them up. On most days, are they smiling and laughing and expressing enthusiasm and enjoyment, or are they consistently moody and dragging their feet? If it's the latter, it may be time to revisit your own motivation for their participation in that activity – as well as your child's.

4. Ensure that your schedule has several 'no goal' times with your child, when you spend quantity time as well as quality time 'alone together' without any internet or technological devices.

Whatever age and stage your child is at, their ability to generate happiness and achieve success is dependent on themselves and their own developed capacity for independent thinking and self-sufficiency, managing their stress and emotions, pursuing a sense of purpose and healthy self-development, and building loving and mutually supportive relationships. The environment that gives a child the tools to develop all these capacities will include a considerable degree of autonomy as well as plenty of opportunities to handle challenges and build resilience.

THE SAFETY FACTOR

Whenever I talk about autonomy and opportunities for challenges, the response I get from my clients is almost always concerns about safety, so I imagine you may be having that concern as well – understandably so. Most parents' own childhood was very different from the way their children are growing up – and maybe just because childhood today is so unrecognisable to them, the average parent today spends a lot more time overseeing their children than their own parents ever spent with them.

This is in part due to issues of safety – whether real or imagined, in response to daily fear-producing stories (often sensationalised) in the media, or health and safety laws that make us over-protective. In all but one state in the USA, a parent can be arrested for allowing their child to play unsupervised. In Florida, the parents of an eleven-year-old were arrested and charged with negligence for letting their son play with a ball alone in their driveway for ninety minutes. A Maryland family has been in the national news, charged for allowing their children aged six and ten to play in a gated playground without supervision. In California, North Carolina, New York and many other states, parents have been charged with negligence for letting their children play the way they themselves played as children: unsupervised, outdoors.

This in spite of the fact that it is safer to be a child today than it was in the 1970s, 1980s or 1990s. Duke University has recorded the state of childhood in the United States since 1975, collecting data from sources such as the Census Bureau, the US Department of Education, and the National Center for Health Statistics, and compiling it in their Child and Youth Well-Being Index.[*] The index, published each year, shows that children are considerably less likely to be victims of violent crime than twenty years ago, and the greatest threat to their health and wellbeing is in fact the threat of obesity and a sedentary lifestyle. A study done in England and Germany of 'children's independent mobility' (defined as 'the freedom of children to travel around their own neighbourhood or city without adult supervision') showed that in England in 1971, 80 per cent of eight to nine year-olds walked home from school alone. By 1990, that had dropped to 19 per cent. In 2010 only 6 per cent were allowed to do so.[†]

---

[*] The Child and Youth Well-Being Index (CWI), Center for Child and Family Policy, Duke University, Durham, North Carolina, yearly based on two indicator years: 1975 and 1985.
[†] Ben Shaw, Ben Fagan-Watson, Andreas Redecker et al., *Children's Independent Mobility: A Comparative Study in England and Germany (1971–2010)* (Policy Studies Institute, 2013).

RISKY PLAY

In this study, the researchers looked at another well-evidenced developmental step that children need to take towards autonomy: engage in play that feels risky.* The researchers and authors of the study concluded that 'Children's engagement in risky play has been associated with a multitude of (positive) developmental, physical and mental health outcomes. Despite this, children's opportunities for risky play show steady decline across generations. Parents' fear and exaggerated perception of risks, such as abduction and traffic injury, are a major deterrent to children's engagement in risky play.'

Despite all the available evidence showing that children are safer than ever, parents are still increasingly anxious and worried about their offspring. This is probably for a variety of reasons – media and our 24/7 access to sensationalised reports, social media fearmongering, increases in litigation, often exaggerated responses by health and safety authorities, our own lack of community or 'village', divorces and custody battles, more single-parent families, and so on – but the actual fact about children's safety is that they are safer than or as safe as they have ever been. However, parents' perceptions are so clouded by externally induced anxiety and the lack of cohesion around them that they lose touch with their own intuitive understanding of their children's developmental needs. The result is anxiety-driven parenting; not allowing their children time on their own (preferably outdoors) to discover some autonomous play and natural outcomes, to create make-believe scenarios with 'kingdoms' and forts and other

* Ellen Beate Hansen Sandseter, 'Scaryfunny: A Qualitative Study of Risky Play among Preschool Children', doctoral thesis (NTNU, 2010).

settings for their imaginary play Instead, parents choose the 'safer' option: the children in their rooms with their devices.

Children, when monitored or constantly watched, do not feel free enough to play spontaneously and un-self-consciously, nor do most today have enough time to explore and learn from risky activities such as climbing trees, banging nails to build a treehouse or cutting cardboard boxes with a pair of scissors or a penknife. (I can almost hear a sharp intake of breath.) Little by little, today's growing degree of parental control can easily prevent children from engaging with opportunities that cultivate their confidence in their own ability for independence. As a result, they themselves develop anxiety in place of a strong sense of self, a problem we are seeing in young adults with alarming escalations.

With this awareness, however, we can instead decide to encourage our child's self-confidence and the building of their resilience by looking for ways to allow them to try out their own capacities without our constant watchful eye. Although there are pockets of parents and other adults working creatively to tackle this issue with more 'free-range' environments and approaches, most countries' health-and-safety laws can make it somewhat of a challenge. Nevertheless, there are initiatives that are growing in popularity such as adventure playgrounds (their locations are easy to find online) and a movement known as Playwork.* I would imagine that many of these are fuelled by intuitive parenting.

* Joan Almon, *Adventure: The Value of Risk in Children's Play* (CreateSpace, 2013); Penny Wilson, *The Playwork Primer* (Alliance for Childhood, 2009).

It is well worth exploring those options for your children if they are available in your area, but it is even more important that you, the parent, manage your own anxieties; understand where those anxieties come from and use the tools outlined in this book to tune into your own intuitive knowledge of your child's needs – and then prioritise your child's development over your own fears and what-ifs. As the song says, 'Letting go is hard to do', but your children really need you to – it's one of the keys to the secure, fulfilled adult you want your child to become and foundational for the development of their healthy self-esteem.

Chapter 8

Giving Unspoken Support
How to listen, fully tuned in

> '*Most people do not listen with the intent to understand; they listen with the intent to reply.*' Stephen R. Covey, *The 7 Habits of Highly Effective People* (Simon & Schuster, 2004)

THE BREAKDOWN OF LISTENING SKILLS

We don't listen. Really, we don't. Listening requires us to be fully present, and if there is one thing that seems to have become increasingly difficult to do, it's to be fully present, and therefore to fully listen. Children complain more about parents not listening to them than they have ever done[*] and the increased pressures of life appear to have shortened our attention spans significantly, reducing our ability to focus on just one thing at a time. If someone who is speaking to us doesn't get straight to the point we lose interest and pull out our phone 'just to check'; we check our devices for social media updates or emails if the film we're watching has a lull in it, and we text while we're giving our child instructions on their schedule, all

---

[*] Sherry Turkle, *Alone Together: Why We Expect More from Technology and Less from Each Other* (Basic Books, 2011); Michael P. Nichols, *The Lost Art of Listening: How Learning to Listen Can Improve Relationships* (Guilford Press, 2009).

the while convincing ourselves that we are really good at multitasking, when what we are actually getting good at is doing nothing very well.

While we have gained convenience and an ease of connecting that we couldn't even dream of a generation ago, we seem to be losing the ability to be fully present with someone, to give all our attention to listening and understanding so that the person feels heard and felt. The erosion of this ability is taking its toll on all relationships, but especially our relationships with our children.

The breakdown of listening as an ability or skill is also evident inside our own minds where we are multitasking while supposedly listening to someone. Although we hear what is being said, we are simultaneously assessing the part that resonated most, even judging it, and framing our own reply while a multitude of other thoughts that have nothing at all to do with the conversation are running rampant in our head: what we're having for dinner, the traffic report, the shopping list we forgot, the missed phone call and all the emails we have to write as soon as we can get back to our device. I certainly cannot listen successfully in this way, nor can anyone else I have ever met, yet we all continue to attempt to listen and multitask simultaneously as if it were actually possible. Then we wonder why we have so many misunderstandings and challenges in our communications and capacity to understand each other.

To truly listen requires attention, willingness to place our own issues aside and respect. It requires that we give the speaker (even if they are just a toddler) our full and focused attentiveness, that we are willing to untether ourselves from any agenda we might have while we listen, and that we respect the speaker enough to consider their expressions seriously. Unfortunately, because this doesn't happen much today, we experience and witness endless frustrations, misinterpretations, misunderstandings, disagreements, arguments and conflicts in every area of life to an extraordinary, and I would posit unmatched, level. In families, corporations, organisations, groups and relationships of every kind, the failure to listen properly is rampant and regrettably also forms the basis of assumptions that underlie many important decisions made on all levels of society – assumptions that were made because we didn't take the time, nor did we have the focus, to listen well.

Fully listening

There are several methods in current practice to attempt to address this, including Active Listening, Nonviolent Communication and various versions of Empathic Listening and Deep Listening, to name the most common.* Effective though all of these are, I have found the most successful foundation for fully listening in any relationship, but particularly for parents, is Creative Listening, a method pioneered by child therapist Dr Rachel Pinney.† She developed her listening

---

* Active Listening has been a popular technique, often taught in corporate settings. It includes internally repeating the words that are being said, and often repeating back the words to the speaker. Personally, I find this method limiting. For Nonviolent Communication, see Marshall B. Rosenberg, *Nonviolent Communication: A Language of Life* (Puddle Dancer Press, 2003).

† Rachel Pinney, *Creative Listening* (The Women's Library Printed Collections, 1981).

techniques while working with children and based them on the principle that total listening cannot be achieved by intention or will alone but by the listener's decision to totally switch off their own views for the duration of the 'listen'. The practice of listening in this way is not easy, but does enable almost anyone to perfect focused attention in listening, however much their opinions differ from the speaker or how great the urge to interrupt would normally be.* I have found it also deepens our capacity for empathic listening, and makes the understanding and appreciation the listener can offer more authentic and effective.

In practice, an example might be a friend or family member who is emotionally unnerved and uncertain about a decision they need to make. The norm would be to offer advice, telling them your viewpoint and what you would do under the same circumstances. If you can switch off the urge to do this and instead give the person in question enough time and space to explore their thoughts and feelings out loud without judgement from you, they will be more likely to access their own insights and discover their solution and next steps within themselves, supported as they are by being listened to without interruption or judgement. Their new understandings or solutions will usually be more appropriate for them than any external advice would be, and whatever learning they might gain from their own insight is more liable to be integrated by their brain than advice given to them by someone else.

---

* Developed in parallel to the client-centred work of psychologist Carl Rogers, Dr Pinney's work differed in that it was designed for person-to-person use, whereas Rogers's was therapist-to-client.

THE PARENTAL KNEE-JERK THAT
PREVENTS FULL LISTENING

I recognise that this process can be seen to be more difficult the more you care about the other person, and particularly with children, because who doesn't have an opinion or agenda when raising a child? When a child is upset, worried or angry for whatever reason, they usually want and need their parent and to be comforted by that parent. Parents, for their part, do not like to see their child in distress, so their instinct will be to tell their child not to worry, or 'Don't cry. It's OK!': in other words, to tell them to stop feeling whatever they are feeling. The problem with this is that the child will think that their emotions are wrong to have, that they shouldn't be feeling them. This can create all manner of negative beliefs about themselves, and not only defeat the purpose the parent intended, but also often make matters worse.

To avoid this parental knee-jerk reaction, having the self-awareness to notice it's about to occur is crucial. When this 'noticing' is followed by the use of the three R's (see Chapter 6) or another self-regulating technique, you will find you naturally 'tune in' to your intuitive understanding of the child's true needs. This tends to lead us all to almost organically setting aside any parental agenda, which is instead replaced by the desire to fully understand the child and that child's experience. The process of listening without an agenda can then be implemented, maybe not easily to start with but given some practice it will feel increasingly natural. Your empathy will naturally become stronger as a result, or at the very least become easier to access once you have the intention to be more empathic.

AGENDA-FREE LISTENING: HOW TO DO IT

Here's a guideline to use until agenda-free listening feels natural and easy to do.

1. First, do not multitask. At the risk of repeating myself, your child will not feel heard if you are checking your phone, making a list, scrolling through emails or chopping vegetables while they speak.

2. Focus in the centre of your chest and slow down your breathing.

3. Stay in the moment. Don't keep an eye on the time. Forget about your own worries and distractions so you can remain fully present.

4. Give your agenda (or 'knee-jerk urge to tell'), a time out. Push pause.

5. Connect to the feeling of love for your child or appreciation for an aspect of your child not related to the issue. For instance, if your child is angry with a family member and your agenda that you set aside is your annoyance with the child's behaviour towards them, focus instead on something benign, for example something physical like the child's curly hair or cute freckles. This can help you to stay agenda-free while you listen.

6. Feel your love or appreciation physically in your chest or heart area.

7. Offer empathy – acknowledge and validate your child's feelings. For example: 'You're really angry, I can see that. I am sure you have good reason to be. Tell me about it.' Or, 'You

are very disappointed. That's understandable. I would be too, in your shoes!' Or, 'You really want that play with that toy, right? It feels so awful to not get what you want and to see someone else get it. I know how upsetting that feels!' Then allow your child to express what they are feeling, without any interruptions from you until they have finished.

8. At this point the episode may be resolved or your child will move to resolve it themselves. This often happens when a child feels understood and supported by a parent. If this is not the case, however, help them move to finding a resolution, again without any agenda on your part. For instance, 'How do you think you could handle that now?' Or, 'What could you say to make this all better?' Or, 'What can you think of that will make you feel better?' Then wait and allow your child to reach a resolution on their own. Your only input is non-judgemental encouragement and empathic support. No interruptions to comment or 'tell'.

9. If the expressions and retelling are long and there is no simple way forward, you might want to offer your child the essence of what you heard them say, in a few empathically summarising sentences. At the very least, this can help them feel understood and supported. It is important to note here that with empathy I do not mean sentimental sympathy. You do not want your child to feel like a victim but rather emotionally supported and able to process their experience towards a resolution.

Agenda-free listening can also be helpful in encouraging your child to talk about problems they may otherwise not want to share for fear of being judged or corrected. A structured and managed approach such as this can ensure that your child feels fully listened to and 'tuned into', fully felt, generally. This will also, over time, be a demonstration to your children of how to regulate their own internal state and be empathic listeners – an invaluable life skill, which is supported by recent developments in neuroscience that conclusively show that the sense of attuned connection of which we are capable happens because we are neuro-biologically wired to respond to emotional signals from others.[*] Significantly, research has shown that, when we communicate, words are actually only 7 per cent of what the listener takes in. Of the remaining 93 per cent, 38 is the tone of voice and 55 is non-verbal, which includes body language and our emotional state.[†] I also believe the emotional state of the listener is key, and the more we are masters of our emotional state, the better equipped we are to listen and understand our children – and others – well.

UNSEEN AND UNSPOKEN SUPPORT

You may also want to consider the idea of unseen and unspoken support for whenever your child is having difficulty with something and you are not with them to listen or to encourage. To first overcome any feelings you may have of helplessness or worry, try taking

---

[*]   Naomi I. Eisenberger and Matthew D. Lieberman, 'Why it Hurts to Be Left Out', research paper (University of California, Dept of Psychology, 2004); Matthew D. Lieberman, *Social: Why Our Brains Are Wired to Connect* (Penguin, 2014).

[†]   Albert Mehrabian, *Nonverbal Communication* (Routledge, 2017, first published 1972).

a moment to be still and focus on your own internal state. Check your breath, your posture and the centre of your chest. Slow down your breathing, open your chest and connect with your love for your child, allowing yourself to feel the sensation of it in your heart area. Allow yourself to appreciate your child and then smile. Imagine your love radiating out from your heart to your child, and back to you. Allow yourself to feel good, and imagine how good it may make your child feel. You do not have to be within close proximity of your child to do this, nor do you have to wait until your child is having a problem. Try doing it on a regular basis and see if you can monitor the effect it has on your child and whether it makes a difference to your relationship.

Many studies have been done on the effects of techniques such as distance healing, prayer and healing intention on recipients situated at significant distances from the 'senders'. These studies have had mixed results, although there is evidence of improvements, most specifically on the autonomic nervous system of the 'receivers'.[*] There is also some conclusive evidence for the improvements experienced by receivers being enhanced by their knowledge that they were being 'sent healing' (as opposed to those that did not know).[†] This and other studies would seem to validate my assertion that radiating loving support to our children can be beneficial (but it could be

[*] Marilyn Schlitz et al., 'Distant Healing of Surgical Wounds', *Explore*, vol. 8, no. 4 (2012).
[†] Alison Easter, 'The Efficacy of Distance Healing Intentionality', research paper (University of Edinburgh, 2004).

more beneficial if your child knows about it).* Regardless, there is definitely evidence – and increasingly so in the field of quantum physics – supporting the idea that everything, including our thoughts, emotions and physiology, is energy and that the energy of thought and emotion is particularly potent. As such, 'sending' loving energy can't possibly hurt and might be worth a try.

* Daniel J. Benor, 'Distant Healing', *Subtle Energies & Energy Medicine*, vol. 11, no. 3 (2000); Dean Radin et al., 'Distant Healing Intention Therapies: An Overview of the Scientific Evidence', *Global Advances in Health and Medicine*, vol .4 supplement (2015).

Chapter 9

Letting Go
Staying tuned in during stress, conflict and adolescence

'*What a child doesn't receive, he can seldom later give.*' P. D.
James, *Time to Be in Earnest* (Faber & Faber, 1999)

DEBUNKING A MYTH ABOUT PARENTING ADOLESCENTS

There are many myths about adolescence and what happens to the
teenage brain during those crucial years before fully fledged adulthood
is achieved (all very succinctly described by Daniel Siegel in his book
Brainstorm*). The most disparaging myth relating to intuitive parenting assumes that the teenage years are a time when our children need
us less and less. If we don't stay connected to our intuition and instead
adopt such an idea, it can easily lead us, however unwittingly, to with-
draw from our adolescent and listen to them less, particularly in any
agenda-free way, when in fact this stage of life is when our child really
needs our insightful, intuitive parenting more than ever.

Adolescence (recently established by neuroscientists to last from
about the age of twelve to twenty-four) is a time when all young

---

*   Daniel J. Siegel, *Brainstorm: The Power and Purpose of the Teenage Brain*
(Jeremy P. Tarcher, 2013).

people need us to use our intuition – by now heightened and strengthened by years of parenting them – to tune in to their underlying needs and experiences with empathy, flexibility and wisdom. Often crucially, they need us to overcome what can be the most challenging time of our parenting experiences. As we feel confused by their unpredictable and sometimes belligerent behaviour, we are not as automatically motivated to be empathic in the way we used to be, and it can become more of a challenge to be understanding while keeping the boundaries most important to us as parents. We may find ourselves losing our temper more often or, conversely, in our wish to avoid confrontation it can be easier to just ignore something we would normally be up in arms over, neither of which is necessarily very helpful.

Letting go does mean gradually allowing more autonomy and responsibility as your child grows through adolescence into young adulthood. But it does *not* mean becoming your child's pal. You are and will always be their parent, which is exactly what they need you to be as they veer from independence to childhood and back to independence, one minute acting as if they have no need for you and the next behaving as if they were a young child. This is when you as a parent are required to be more tuned in than ever, staying connected – even in unspoken and unseen ways – accepting and appreciating your child's unique blossoming, so you can stay open to whatever that might be while still setting the limits you deem necessary, remaining their guide with coherence and consistency. Because adolescent behaviour can often be irrational and unpredictable, it is almost imperative for the parent to remain internally entrained, tuned in to your own intuitive wisdom and predictable in sustaining the boundaries of your core values.

Working out how and when to set limits

One former client of mine – a single mother I shall call Jane – sought me out again because her fourteen-year-old son Josh was, as she put it, 'out of control!' He had been coming home late, not keeping his commitments and being increasingly sassy and rude towards his mother. His grades were lower than ever and he had skipped school on several occasions.

These were all manifestations of what one might expect of a teenager as their brain development moves through the adolescent phase of increased impulsiveness and drive towards rebellion, thrill-seeking and experimental behaviour. The positive aspect of this phase is the daring to transform, to innovate, to explore – all qualities that diminish as we age but which propel us forward as a species. It is at this time of life that the brain's capacity to understand what it means to be one part of a greater whole, how to fit into the larger world, emerges and becomes assimilated. Simultaneously, the adolescent is progressing towards emotional separation and the expression of their identity, establishing their distinctive and eventually adult self. This growth period is complex, long, often occurs in fits and spurts, and can feel messy. It naturally involves pushing away from and testing the boundaries of both parents and society.

Josh's testing of boundaries was natural but also an opportunity to gauge some consequences of his behaviour. His mother's

permissive response, however, merely showed him that her boundaries were weak, possibly teaching him that the boundaries were
unreliable (and therefore not safe) or that bullying behaviour was
acceptable. Once Jane had described the situation to me, it also
became evident that she had allowed her son to get away with
behaviour that in her own mind was unacceptable. She had set
boundaries and what she called 'home rules' but had been inconsistent in enforcing them, giving in to Josh's nagging and defiance.
Having the desire to be a 'cool mum' and a friend to her son, she
had basically relinquished her role as his guiding parent, allowing
him to cross her 'bottom line' of what was acceptable to her as his
mother. The result was that not only had Josh become 'out of
control', but they no longer had the close, earnest conversations
Jane had nurtured that meant so much to her, and that would in
fact teach Josh the self-reflection so sorely needed by any adolescent navigating this difficult time.

As soon as she understood what she had allowed to happen, Jane
mapped out a plan for change. She began by reconnecting with her
core values that she had imparted to Josh when he was small but
which she had let slide in recent years. She continued by writing
down her home rules and how they aligned with her core values, and
then went through them with Josh in a calm, reflective conversation,
ensuring she was managing her own emotions. After explaining her
reasons and values behind the rules she asked for his input and, to
her surprise, he was in complete agreement. In the weeks that
followed Jane worked on using her skills to stay internally entrained
and was consistent in sticking to her rules. She ensured that consequences were carried out when Josh broke the rules (including being

rude and disrespectful). In short, she held him responsible for his actions and behaviour.

After a few initial protests (followed by her quiet but firm reminders of his agreement and the positive values he also held), Josh adjusted and they soon had a much more amiable relationship, with long chats over the dinner table reinstated and a mutually respectful tone. Jane was delighted with her regained role as 'the parent' and, when I asked Josh whether he thought there had been improvement, he grinned and replied, 'It's cool to know I have a mum who loves me enough to call me on my shit!'

Knowing when and how to set your limits requires you as a parent to hold the 'north star' of your core values for your child while staying tuned into your child's needs. Then, to communicate the limits in a managed, clear, respectful way, acknowledging your child's good intentions if possible (e.g. how thoughtful of them to want to drive their friends to a rock concert) while helping them stay focused on the positive alternatives and realistic outcomes (e.g. not driving may result in more ease and fun, as they may be likely to be tempted to drink). This can seem like a tall order but becomes less so when you stay internally coherent, centred and connected to your intuition.

While adolescence is all about reaching outside the box, experimenting and innovating, as a parent it may be tempting to forget this and criticise your child for attitudes or actions that are in essence a natural and necessary stage in the process of growing up. It is also easy to become defensive if your teenager blames you for their problems or yells at you in anger. You may feel justifiably hurt. Nevertheless, it is important to use your self-management skills to stay objective and 'tuned in'. Silently acknowledge your emotions to yourself and take responsibility for managing them. Avoid adding to the tension by projecting your emotions onto the situation. Remind yourself that whatever the problem is, it will be solved. Your child may be just doing what nature intended – individuating. That's their 'job'. Your job as a parent is to create and sustain a safe environment, physically, mentally and emotionally, for them to blossom into their own unique self. You do this best by communicating mindfully, listening uncon-ditionally, honouring your child's increasing creativity, positive power and innovation, even if it sometimes seems crazy to you, and setting limits that they can connect to their values and positive outcomes.

It is always worth remembering that you cannot control the person your adolescent is becoming; the best you can do is to ensure the lines of communication stay open so you continue to play an impor-tant role in your young adult's life. Communicating in a mindful, authentically respectful manner is essential, even when it seems insurmountably challenging.

Conflict, anyone?

There's bound to be conflict. As your child grows, there will be moments when either you or your child are critical, defensive or aggressive. Whether this is because your child is non-compliant or in the process of exploring and asserting their individuality, or you are over-stretched and stressed, it is likely at some point as your child finds their own identity independent of you. In all cases, how you handle conflict will have an immense influence on the outcome. Should you try to avoid all conflict by doing as my client Jane did, allowing your child's emotional behaviour to determine what happens, you'll only generate additional angst and uneasiness and find yourself even less willing to make waves. This eventually creates a stress-fuelled cycle that, while understandable, may not serve anybody in the long run. If, on the other hand, your adolescent is withdrawn and conflict-avoidant, you as the parent may feel the urge to pressurise them into communicating. Unfortunately, the more a parent coerces their teen, the more avoidant they are likely to become. Another unhelpful cycle.

The natural process of individuation means the young person is seeking to create a life and tribe of their own, which means increasing interactions with their peer group while exploring their own educational, occupational and personal goals that will define them as a young adult, independently from their parents. While this is natural, it can also create or exacerbate conflict with parents who may resent having less and less authority or even a say. This is such a common phenomenon that as a society we tend to conclude that conflict is inevitable. My experience, however, is that while some friction may be normal, full-blown conflict is not necessary.

I have long been aware of the many studies on parent–child conflict, but when looking into the research, I found that not only have a diverse array of studies been done on the subject of parent–child conflict, but they have also looked specifically at cultural differences, and been carried out in multiple countries.* I find this particularly interesting because, in my coaching practice, it is in parent–child conflict that I have found cultural considerations to make the greatest differences in how we raise our children. One of the most distinguishing areas among different cultures is *confrontational conflict* versus *conflict avoidance*. It is an important consideration to make because, as a parent, your attitude to conflict is linked to your culture, your family of origin (how you were raised) and your values.

Try this:

It is worthwhile for all parents to explore and establish an attitude to conflict. Take some time and space and sit down with a pen and paper and write a response to each of the following questions:

- How do you ideally view conflict (aligned with your values)?
- How was conflict addressed in your own upbringing and culture? (And do you consciously wish to follow the same path or to diverge from it and create your own way?)
- How do you currently do conflict?

The listening method outlined in Chapter 8 can be helpful as a significant step in resolving conflict rather than avoiding it or letting it

---

* José Rubén Parra-Cardona et al., 'Epidemiological Research on Parent–Child Conflict in the United States', *PeerJ* (24 January 2017); Qin Zhang, 'Family Communication Patterns and Conflict Styles in Chinese Parent–Child Relationships', *Communication Quarterly*, vol. 55, no. 1 (2007); Rashmi Singh and Jogendra Kumar Nayak, 'Parent–Adolescent Conflict and Choice of Conflict Resolution Strategy', *International Journal of Conflict Management*, vol. 27, no. 1 (2016).

cause family ruptures. The tuning in that agenda-free listening requires you to do will help you with the first step – however hard it may be sometimes – which is to accept differences, and particularly to keep in mind that your child is individuating and will develop their own ideas, goals and relationships, which will not always meet your approval.

Both for ourselves and our child's development, if we can manage our emotions so our brain stays switched on and tuned in, we will be more mindful and better able to keep our three levels of influence aligned with our values – and any values issues within the conflict as well as with how we really *want* to parent. In many cases, it can help us see our child's point of view and recognise the merit of their argument. Once they feel validated it will increase the likelihood of finding compromises that improve collaboration and understanding on both sides. Notably, it is often within a conflict that we capture the differences and diversity that ultimately make the family a strong unit. If we can embrace that idea, we may even gain insights into how we can improve our communication as parents, generally.

YOUR IMAGE OF YOUR CHILD OR ADOLESCENT

I have explored communication from several angles so far, as it is such a pivotal aspect of parenting; when we get it right we are invariably tuned in and coherent; when we get it wrong, we are usually in stress with a brain occupied by images of negativity.

What is the image you hold of your child or adolescent – and their behaviour? You have probably experienced that it can depend on how you feel, on your emotion in the moment. When we reflect back on a parenting communication that we regret and would like to have done differently, exploring the image we held of our child at that time can help us understand the accompanying emotion, and then reframe it. Were there judgements involved? Did we *expect* unruly behaviour?

When we are anxious that our child will have a public meltdown, or we envisage them being disruptive, uncommunicative or unmanageable, chances are they probably will be, because the image we have of them creates an expectancy which in turn drives how we communicate; either we are incongruent (our three levels are not entrained) or we are communicating in a way that clearly shows what kind of image we hold of them and what we expect. The same is of course true of the reverse; when we tune in to our child's capacity for kindness and the resulting image is of a considerate child, the likelihood of them behaving that way is increased as you communicate with that image and anticipation in mind.

Try this:

Whatever your child's age, take a moment – while you're driving, cleaning or gardening are good moments – to hold an image of your child in the near future. It could be later that same day, the next day or in a week's time. Imagine their response to something specific, a behavioural challenge maybe. Imagine it as positive and as perfect for them as you can. See them responding with ease and a resulting satisfaction, contentment or happiness. Make your image as vivid as you can. Include colours, sounds, tastes and smells. Focus on the perfect scenario and *expect* it to happen.

If your mind projects a more negative scenario, replace it with the perfect, positive one, and try to hold it for as long as you can. Put your heart into it, fuelling it with feelings of appreciation for your child. Repeat this as often as you can.

When the time comes, should your child not react exactly as you had visualised, do not let yourself slip into becoming disappointed. Tune in and focus instead on whatever positive qualities or growth opportunities you can find in the situation and encourage your child with what you see.

You may also find this process helpful if you are planning to have a difficult conversation with your adolescent that is part of an ongoing conflict or that you are concerned may develop into a conflict. In order to stay tuned in to yourself, your child and your parenting intuition, approaching the interaction without a preconceived negative image will make a big difference.

YOUR STRESS IN CONFLICT

There is no time in our parenting journey when stress gets more in the way of our intuitive parenting wisdom than when we're in conflict with our child. All the approaches and suggestions throughout this book to help you deepen your connection to that wisdom, to tune in to yourself and your child, will be tested when you have a belligerent adolescent in front of you challenging your authority and triggering your default stress response to the max. When that time comes, it will be helpful if you have become aware of and identified your trigger, where you 'parent from stress' most readily, and also if you've given some attention to taking charge of that 'default'. One client of mine calls it 'parent self-awareness 101'. Whatever age and stage your child is at, knowing your 'parenting-in-stress' default style is key both when it comes to conflict and to communication in general.

I encourage you to reflect on the following list and note which one resonates with you and the style you default to when in stress. Make a commitment to catch yourself and interrupt yourself when doing it. Use the three R's (Recognise, Release, Reframe – see Chapter 6) if need be, and you will soon find it stops being a default. When that happens, celebrate!

PARENTING-IN-STRESS DEFAULT BEHAVIOURS

1. Threatening
2. Being defensive
3. Criticising
4. Lecturing
5. Catastrophising
6. Fixing and rescuing
7. Guilt (either acting from guilt or laying guilt on)
8. Shaming
9. Cramming morals
10. Trying to make control look like it's 'for their own good'
11. Withdrawing love or attention
12. Confusing behaviour with identity

Managing the terrain of parent–child individuation and potential conflict is, I believe, both an art and a science. The experience we have raising our child before it gets to that point should be helpful, but it is only when we drop into our own intuition and access our deep insights into who that emerging young adult is, in their essence, that we access what really feels right for guiding this young person we love so much.

Chapter 10

Intuitive Parenting
Listening to yourself

> 'If there is anything we wish to change in a child, we should first
> examine it and see whether it is not something that could be better
> changed in ourselves.' Carl Jung, *Collected Works: Vol. 17 – On the*
> *Development of Personality* (Princeton University Press, 1954)

I began this book by lamenting the usurping of parent intuition by
the overwhelming amount of 'expert' information available and I
fully recognise the irony in adding yet another book to this copious
mass. I don't for one moment imagine that it will solve the whole
problem, especially the dilemma of our media-addicted 'tuning out'
from each other and our children, but I do hope it will contribute to
the growing movement for taking back control of our own autonomous thinking, and empowering parents to 'tune in' more to their
own wisdom. Most of all, I hope that those of you who pick up this
book will be helped to develop a deeper connection with your intuition and take charge of the stress that has prevented you from building your confidence in the power of your own intuitive conviction –
especially your parenting intuition.

Listening to your intuition, whether parenting or otherwise, can be
said to be the same as listening to your heart (as long as you are

conscious of not confusing the heart with an overemotional or sentimental response), fuelled as intuition is by unconditional love, and
by the sense of rightness, presence and ultimately conviction that is
the result of our heart, body and brain being in harmony. Once tuned
into and acted upon, intuition is a powerful force. Not only does it
give us insights into our self and our child, but it also strengthens the
sense of a 'north star', helping us to choose which expert advice is the
right one for us in those moments when we do need to access
expertise.

BEING, DOING AND HAVING

Even when we know this about our intuition, tuning into it first
rather than looking for answers outside ourselves may still be a challenge, because tuning in is the opposite of the default reaction to any
issue in a society where we are 'programmed' to look outside of
ourselves in order to get answers, or whatever it is that we need.
Unfortunately, more often than not we will keep looking, never fully
satisfied.

It reminds me of the oft-quoted doing-having-being concept: that we
are typically encouraged to 'do' whatever we must do in order to
'have' what we want to have in order to 'be' happy, when in actual fact
this is not how the human species is designed at all. Rather, we function best when we turn this concept around: we must first 'be' in
order to know what we need to 'do' so we can 'have' what we desire.
We will only be fulfilled, satisfied or feel right with what we have
when what we do to attain it is an expression of who we are; our
beliefs, our values, our delights and our outrage.

Only when we can *be* the unique being each one of us is – when we know our own strengths and weaknesses, what gives us joy and sorrow, what is important to us, what are our natural talents and predispositions, and we are in tune with our intuition, with what drives us – will we have a strong, sustainable foundation to *do* what we do best – whether as parents or otherwise – with clarity, focus and a sense of purpose. It is at this point that we will find we *have* or can easily draw to us what we want – or we find we are happy and gratified with what we already have.

This state of 'being' – a tuned-in state – is also one of the greatest gifts we can offer our child. We give this gift most effectively when we are aware that, like a pebble dropped into a lake, all that we feel, say and do has a ripple effect. When that ripple effect comes from a tuned-in state, it not only means better parenting but is also more likely to be an example of 'how to be in the world', and an example that you *want* to set.

In conclusion

I'd like to leave you with an 'Intuition Index', an abridged reminder of how to get into and sustain that tuned-in state of being and parenting. Whenever you find yourself *not* already in that tuned-in state or questioning why you are not fully trusting your intuition, bear in mind that the best place to begin moving yourself into the intuitive state will always be to look first at what is getting in the way. The following pages give you a brief summary of the main culprits we have looked at, for you to use as a shortcut to addressing whichever applies to you. The more often you tackle your particular issue the easier it will become to reduce its hold on you.

The summary is followed by the Keys to Intuitive Parenting, an index of the key tools for tuning in to yourself and your child, and strengthening your confidence in your intuitive parenting. Hopefully the more you use this information the more often you'll find yourself going straight to those tools, with less and less need to spend time on whatever issue has been getting in the way.

WHAT GETS IN THE WAY

Stress

Stress, as we know, is the most effective impediment of the full and proper functioning of the part of the brain needed for any wise and intuitive insights, as the amygdala kicks in to initiate our self-defence mechanism against perceived threat. Often aptly referred to as an 'amygdala hijack', it is particularly insidious when it remains at that initial stage, the low-grade stress that is not necessarily visible but is constantly with us like background noise, never fully bringing our stress reaction into conscious awareness and so making it easy to disregard – much like we might inadvertently disregard a quiet child as opposed to one who throws loud tantrums.

When we typically think of stress (or *dis*-stress as opposed to *eu*-stress), the images we conjure up are likely to be of recognisably detrimental emotions. We tend to associate the word stress with petulant behaviour, sometimes frantic energy or at least visible edginess. Yet as parents we will likely experience the more common state of ongoing low-grade stress – invisible but nevertheless releasing the stress hormone cortisol continuously into our system like a dripping tap – persistently inhibiting our intuition in addition to increasing our feelings of insecurity and inadequacy.

Prompts:

1. Your self-awareness is key. Tie a piece of string around your wrist to increase your awareness.
2. Notice whether you are parenting-in-stress. Check the parenting-in-stress list in Chapter 9.
3. Initiate the 'Find the Feeling' game with your family (see Chapter 6 and the Appendix). Naming emotions is the first step to managing stress.
4. When you notice tension in your body, exhale and release the tension, physically. Clench your fist then splay out your hands. Shake your hands, run or jump.
5. Then take three slow breaths. Focus your attention in your heart area as you lengthen the exhale.
6. If need be, have a family tantrum.
7. Use humour.

There but not there

Technology advances very fast, and months if not years will have passed since I wrote this book. But no matter how long it's been, the fact will remain that technology is not human and, no matter how sophisticated it becomes, it will never replace the fully present, loving and nurturing connection that every child needs from their parent or primary caregiver. The secure attachment developed from your fully present, connected parenting forms the foundation for the wellbeing and healthy relationships of your child's future.

How parents manage children's use of technology is relentlessly discussed in the media and by authorities researching that field, and it really is a whole other book. Suffice to say, children will learn first and foremost from a parent's demonstration and example. Being aware that the 'loss of the village' may also be playing a part can help you establish ways to prioritise real connection in as many forms as possible.

Prompts:

1. Ensure you are fully present with your child when communicating. Put down your device and connect, two eyes to two eyes.

2. Each morning before checking any device, breathe deeply and connect with a feeling of appreciation for your child. Really feel it.

3. No screens or devices in children's bedrooms, nor in any bedroom. They interfere with sleep as well as quality of rest.

4. No screens at the dinner table or when you go out to eat. Aside from being detrimental to the digestive system, they rob you of the opportunity to share stories and experiences (needed for strengthening your relationships for the future), and they also rob you of opportunities to teach your child vital social skills.

5. Take time every day to be with your child, with 100 per cent fully focused attention. Switch off all devices and connect. Listen. Share. Enjoy.

6. When waiting to meet your child, meditate on your love and appreciation for them rather than checking your phone.

(Ask yourself: what will you be regretting on your deathbed?)

7. Whenever you reconnect with your child, really connect with them with your full and complete present self, even if it's just for two minutes.

Expectations

The expectations we have of our child that can get in the way of our parenting intuition are those expectations that are not aligned with the innate and true nature of our child, and so are essentially unrealistic – and, indeed, often negatively impact our relationship with our child. If not addressed, those expectations unmet will lead to emotional disappointments that limit our brain's ability for clear, intuitive thinking and ultimately can in turn limit our child's progress.

Such unrealistic expectations can be due to any number of different reasons, which you may want to explore and understand. Ultimately, however, it is your self-awareness as a parent that will let you know whether you are experiencing stress that is not aligned with your child and with helping them develop a growth mindset rather than living up to stress-producing expectations. Managing your expectations and the accompanying pressure means recognising that your brain is creating emotions that are unhelpful and interfering with your intuition.

Prompts:

1. Take ten minutes with a pen and paper and write about any disappointment you have in your child, their behaviour,

choices or achievements. Use the three R's (Recognise, Release, Reframe) from Chapter 6 to help you gain a wider perspective.

2. Make a list of all the qualities you appreciate about your child. Feel your appreciation. Focus on three things from this appreciation list every morning

3. Reference the brain's integration process (Chapter 5) and use it to help you 'meet' your child where they are, mentally and emotionally.

4. When your child behaves in ways that are hurtful or otherwise unacceptable, validate your child's emotions first or as soon as possible. All feelings are valid. It is their expression that may be inappropriate.

5. Separate your child's behaviour from who they are. Notice your own language and adjust it so you correct unacceptable behaviour rather than identity (for example, shift from saying 'You are . . .' to 'Your behaviour is . . .').

6. Help your child reframe and explore a better way to behave.

7. Guide your child to develop a growth mindset: avoid over-praising and instead praise and encourage effort and engagement.

Over-parenting

Parental concern and enthusiasm can easily become intrusive and disempowering. No matter how much you love your child, if you are over-parenting you may be driven by meeting your own needs whereas your child needs your support to be focused on their needs. Over involvement and over-parenting will likely lead to anxiety and insecurity in your child. Bear in mind that the purpose of most of your child's activities is the development of self-reliance, and this is a desire your child will always have (as we all do).

A parent's role is especially significant when it comes to relationships. Hanging out, face to face, with no goal in mind, allows time and connection for a loving relationship to be fully experienced and developed. Being together without needing to have any activity or achievement allows your child to feel safe and unconditionally loved for just being who they are. When a strong relationship has been built and your child feels unconditionally loved and trusted to be self-reliant, parental letting go, although one of the hardest things for any parent to do, is a healthy process that feels intuitively right.

Prompts:
1. Avoid over-scheduling. Choose extra-curricular activities according to your intuitive insights into your child as well as your child's expressed desires.
2. When you schedule activities and extra-curricular commitment for your child, ensure there is regular weekly time to 'just hang out'.
3. When you have a quiet moment, ask yourself if your child's schedule is balanced. Are your aspirations in the picture? If so, is it time to let them go?
4. Consult your child about their activities. Listen to their input. Notice their emotions.
5. Ensure your child's environment gives them plenty of opportunities to experience becoming capable, able to manage their own stress and to think independently.

6. Allow your child to engage with opportunities to take non-hazardous risks and generally meet challenges, without your constant watchful eye.

7. Manage your own stress and anxiety around your child's emerging independence.

INTUITION INDEX: KEYS TO INTUITIVE PARENTING

Three levels of influence

Given that we influence our children and indeed everyone around us on three levels – our self-awareness, our imagery and language – it really is unsurprising that complications in communications are so common. If our emotions are not congruent with our words or our actions, we will inevitably come across as inauthentic, no matter how good we think we are at covering up our true feelings. Because your children are more sensitive to you than most others, ensuring that your three levels of influence and communication are congruent and aligned will help you stay connected to your intuition and tuned in to your child. Managing your emotions is probably the most critical key to sustaining this.

If the words we use are expressions of emotions that we are not fully aware of having, we inadvertently create beliefs in our child that will impact their self-image. For example, if we feel frustrated with ourselves for not planning enough time to complete all the errands that need to be done, we may, instead of managing our own feelings and thoughts, lash out at our son for taking his jolly time to get dressed with 'Why can't you get dressed quickly like your brother? What's wrong with you? You're always so damned slow!' Instead, we can notice our own tension, be aware of our own underlying frustration and self-criticism, and say to ourselves, 'This is just an emotion my brain is creating', followed by a kinder encouragement of our child, tuning into his needs and speaking from a more intuitive state. We can take charge of how we say things first of all by being aware and mindful of our own emotional state and taking responsibility for that, and secondly by becoming more mindful of our words and their effect.

The more self-aware we are, the more tuned in to our actions we become – the more tuned in we are to what we do and demonstrate to our child. In Chapter 3, I suggested drawing up a list of the behaviours you believe are important for your child to embody and, next to each behaviour, what might be getting in the way of you behaving or acting that way yourself. You may have discovered that some of your own behaviours and actions need to be adjusted to become more aligned to your values. I encourage you to keep checking in with this process regularly – it's a powerful tool.

Prompts:

1. Entrainment – keep it in mind. Putting a photo of an entrained flock of birds on your desktop or phone can be a helpful reminder of this concept, and help you focus on your own state to create the coherent entrainment you want.

2. Take a parent time-out to help you create entrainment. Whether it's just a mental time out or it's safe for you to go to the bathroom on your own, always let your child know you will be right back to connect. Breathe, let your tension

go and focus on a benign thing you can appreciate. Feel the appreciation. You've got this!

3. Communicate authentically – then take responsibility for correcting what's not working. Use the three R's to help you.

4. If your child witnesses an argument, let them also witness the making up and any apologies.

5. Use a notebook to increase your self-awareness – particularly of your spoken language.

6. Use the list of behaviours to check in with yourself and your example, especially when you are annoyed with any repeated behaviour of your child.

7. Practise tuning in to yourself each and every morning, even if it's only with three slow breaths.

Core-values blueprint

The integrated awareness of your core values into your life and parenting gives you a blueprint or 'north star' for your intuitive parenting. Your core values create an anchor for your child and for you. Parenting and living according to your core values as much as possible will in itself eliminate stress to a significant degree and make your intuition simpler to access.

As your child grows, you may find them adopting one or two core values of their own that are not at the top of your list. This is quite normal, and it can be important for them that you validate their choices. Ensuring that the values you hold most dear are integrated into your child's life and behaviours will be helped by a clear awareness of those values in your family.

Prompts:

1. Create an 'Our Family Values' chart together.
2. Reference the values both when they are violated and when they are expressed or manifested in an action.
3. The encouragement of core values is key to their integration.
4. Notice, whenever you feel upset, angry or stuck in stress mode, whether one of your values has been or is being violated – by yourself or another.
5. Whenever you notice a core value being violated or encroached upon, especially by yourself, give yourself some time and space to tune into yourself and explore how and why it happened.
6. Use the three R's to help you find the best way – a way that is aligned with your values – to address or correct the encroachment.
7. Use your core values as your blueprint to help you pick your battles and set boundaries that are the most important to you.

The three R's of managing emotions and accessing intuition

Managing your emotions is, at the risk of repeating myself, probably the most important and helpful element of tuning into yourself and tuning into your child. It is the doorway to intuitive parenting and central to overcoming all the obstacles that get in the way. Practice is the key to that doorway. Use the three R's – Recognise, Release, Reframe – regularly and especially at the end of your day to help you process and work through the issues of the day. If you need to pick just one practice from this book to work on, choose the three R's.

Prompts:

1. Recognise: What are you feeling? Where in your body is the associated tension?

2. Carry around a small notebook and note your emotions down, as well as where in your body each one registers. It will get you into the habit of tuning in to your body and your feelings, and you'll start to notice what they do to your thinking.

3. Play the 'Find the Feeling' game with your family (see Chapter 6). It will not only help increase each person's awareness but also allow everyone to have an equal emotional voice, and you may even see empathy increasing.

4. Release: Once noticed, the tension in your body needs to be released. Exhaling or blowing out can serve this purpose, as can rolling shoulders, shaking your hands out, a silent scream or just releasing the tension in whatever body part you feel it. (See Chapter 6 for more ideas.)

5. Follow this release with three slow breaths, extending the exhale. Count up to four seconds for the inhale and six seconds for the exhale. One hand held lightly over the heart area can be helpful. Encourage your child to practise this breathing technique – using it to centre yourselves as a family (for instance, before mealtimes).

6. Reframe, or relax into a positive emotional state. Allow yourself to activate that inner smile and really feel it. Staying with this feeling will allow your brain to switch on and access your intuitive, wiser perspective. Your fingertips resting gently on your chest will help anchor this state of feeling.

7. Teach your child to access this state as well. It can help to write your insights (or in the case of little ones, to draw). Be sure to give yourself the space to use this tool and you will find yourself needing less and less time for it the more you practise.

Accepting what is

As your child grows, so does their brain and all the neural connections and pathways that will in large part determine the adult they become and the way they learn to navigate their world. Being accepted for who we are, in our true nature, by our parents is widely acknowledged to play a significant role in our emotional health and wellbeing. It also impacts how the brain develops; which neural pathways are strengthened and which are not. The more often a child experiences themselves as 'enough' and loved by their parents for who they are, the more secure they will feel in themselves and the more parents will contribute to them feeling comfortable in themselves. While not the only influence, parents are the most foundational.

Prompts:

1. If you find unconditional acceptance difficult sometimes (and most of us do!), remind yourself to appreciate 'what is' with a picture of different flowers, or something to that effect, in a place you often look. Your phone, desktop or the kitchen wall are good places.

2. Revisit the growth mindset information (Chapter 5) and your own language (Chapter 3) to ensure you are contributing constructively.

3. Remind yourself of the integration process and how the brain learns and integrates information. Ensure you are 'meeting your child where they are'.

4. Make or revisit a list of qualities you appreciate about your child and their uniqueness. Focus on that.

5. Practise breathing slowly and tuning into your intuition each morning before getting up. Ask yourself; 'What is needed of me today?'

6. Use the three R's and your intuition to find the balance between accepting what is and setting boundaries as your child grows, and avoid confusing the two. Take time to talk with your partner or co-parent, if you have one, or reflect in your journal, proactively.

7. Whatever the age of your child, practise holding positive images of them and their actions, imagining that they handle themselves in the best way possible for themselves, whatever that looks like. Fuel the image with appreciation for them and their unique nature. Do not expect a perfect image to unfold in reality, but focus on the positive image for your child and how they handle themselves.

Listening to and empowering your child

As your child grows up, you will enter the parent realm of 'letting go'. This can be challenging and sometimes even painful, but it can also give you many wonderful moments as you witness your child blossoming into the unique and autonomous young adult you have raised. Gradually allowing that autonomy and increasingly more responsibility will, in my experience, require more depth of connection with your intuition, and with the capacity to tune in to the emerging adult before you.

It does not entail that you become your child's buddy no matter how much you may want to! They need you to be their parent. Listening more and 'telling' less is typically required, and backing off while empowering your teen can be a tricky balancing act. Intuitive parenting can be vital at this point in time. When faced with a belligerent, unkempt teenager and finding yourself wondering whatever happened to that cute little curly-haired cherub, your ability to stay emotionally managed and connected to your intuitive wisdom will never have been more imperative.

Whatever age and stage your child is at, listening to and empowering your child will always be beneficial, both as practices that will be increasingly needed as they grow, and as foundational intuitive parenting skills. It bears repeating that truly listening requires your full attention. No phones or devices. Don't do anything else. Just listen – preferably without thinking about your response or any judgements you might otherwise have.

Prompts:

1. If you find yourself having difficulty even though you are fully present, use the three R's, focus on feeling appreciation or just breathe, extending the exhale. Stay tuned in to your centre and your intuitive insights.

2. Step into your child's shoes. How do they see the world? Place your own agenda aside and empathise. Tune into the essence of what your child is telling you. Offer your empathy so they feel understood.

3. Conflict happens. When it does, ensure you are not parenting in stress. Revisit your list and chosen default. Check you are not reverting and, if you are, use the three R's to access that wiser, intuitive you.

4. Adolescence: you cannot control the person your adolescent is becoming – you can only influence them. This you do most effectively by listening and empowering them to arrive at their own wisdom, trusting what you have instilled in them and the true nature of who they are.

5. Your adolescent is meant to be reaching outside their comfort zone. Honour their increasing creativity and innovation. Appreciate what you can and keep lines of communication open.

6. Communicate boundaries and values with love – staying tuned in to yourself and managing your emotions. When you set limits with your teen, ask for their input. Listen.

7. Listen, again. To your child – and then to yourself. Essentially, that *is* intuitive parenting.

Appendix: Find the Feeling Word List

This list is far from exhaustive and is intended for guidance only.

Affectionate	Furious	Mad	Quiet	Surprised
Amused	Gentle	Mean	Radiant	Suspicious
Angry	Grateful	Mellow	Rational	Tender
Anxious	Grumpy	Miserable	Ready	Thankful
Ashamed	Guilty	Mischievous	Rejected	Threatened
Bad	Happy	Mournful	Relaxed	Thoughtful
Bored	Hateful	Muddled	Relentless	Timid
Bothered	Helpful	Nasty	Respected	Tired
Brave	Helpless	Negative	Respectful	Tortured
Clever	Heroic	Nervous	Responsible	Tranquil
Creative	Homesick	Neutral	Restricted	Traumatised
Competent	Hopeless	Noble	Run down	Treasured
Confused	Humorous	Offended	Sad	Troubled
Curious	Hurt	On-guard	Satisfied	Trusting
Delighted	Important	Open	Scared	Trustworthy
Depressed	Innocent	Oppressed	Secure	Unavailable
Determined	Interested	Organised	Sensitive	Uncertain
Disappointed	Intolerant	Overcome	Shocked	Understanding
Dreamy	Insecure	Overjoyed	Shy	Understood
Eager	Inspired	Overwhelmed	Silly	Unhappy
Efficient	Irritable	Passionate	Small	Unique
Embarrassed	Jealous	Peaceful	Smart	Unyielding
Enthusiastic	Jolly	Perplexed	Sophisticated	Upset
Excited	Joyful	Playful	Special	Valued
Flexible	Kind	Pleased	Stressed	Vexed
Focused	Lazy	Precious	Stoic	Volatile
Forgetful	Likeable	Proud	Strong	Warmhearted
Frightened	Lonely	Puzzled	Stuck	Weak
Frustrated	Lovable	Qualified	Stunned	Weird
Funny	Loving	Quarrelsome	Successful	Worried

Bibliography

CHAPTER 1

Sources

Siegel, Daniel J., *The Developing Mind* (Guilford Press, 1999).
Siegel, Daniel J. and Payne Bryson, Tina, *The Whole Brain Child* (Delacorte Press, 2011).

Recommended further reading

Siegel, Daniel J. and Hartzell, Mary, *Parenting from the Inside Out* (Jeremy P. Tarcher/Penguin, 2014; first edition 2003).
Sunderland, Margot, *The Science of Parenting* (DK Publishing, 2006).

CHAPTER 2

Sources

Turkle, Sherry, *Alone Together: Why We Expect More from Technology and Less from Each Other* (Basic Books, 2011).
—, 'Always-on/Always-on-You: The Tethered Self', in Katz, James E. (ed.), *Handbook of Mobile Communication Studies* (MIT Press, 2008).

Recommended further reading

Kardaras, Nicholas, *Glow Kids: How Screen Addiction Is Hijacking our Kids and How to Break the Trance* (St Martin's Press, 2016).

CHAPTER 3
Sources

Feldman, Ruth et al., 'Mother and Infant Coordinate Heart Rhythms through Episodes of Interaction Synchrony', *Infant Behavior and Development*, vol. 34, no, 4 (2011).

LeDoux, Joseph, *The Emotional Brain* (Simon & Schuster, 1996).

LeDoux, J. and Brown, R., 'A Higher Order Theory of Emotional Consciousness', *Proceedings of the National Academy of Sciences* (February 2017).

Levine, Madeline, 'Raising Successful Children', *New York Times* (4 August 2012).

McCraty, R., 'The Energetic Heart: Bioelectromagnetic Communication Within and Between People', in Rosch, P. J. and Markov, M. S. (eds), *Clinical Applications of Bioelectromagnetic Medicine* (Marcel Dekker, 2004).

Morris, S. M., 'Achieving Collective Coherence: Group Effects on Heart Rate Variability Coherence', *Alternative Therapies in Health; Medicine*, vol. 16, no. 4 (2010).

Provenzi, Livio, 'Mother–Infant Dyadic Reparation', *Journal of Experimental Child Psychology*, vol. 140 (2015).

Rosch, P. J. and Markov, M. S. (eds), *Clinical Applications of Bioelectromagnetic Medicine* (Marcel Dekker, 2004).

Will, Udo et al., 'Pulse and Entrainment to Non-Isochronous Auditory Stimuli', *PloS One* (7 April 2015).

Recommended further reading

Childre, Doc Lew, Martin, Howard and Beech, Donna, *The HeartMath Solution* (HarperCollins, 1999).

Day, Jennifer, *Children Believe Everything You Say: Building Self-Esteem with Children* (Element Books, 1997).

CHAPTER 4

Sources

Hayes, S. C., Strosahl, K. and Wilson, K. G., *Acceptance and Commitment Therapy* (Guilford Publications, 1999).

Siegel, Daniel J., *Brainstorm: The Power and Purpose of the Teenage Brain* (Jeremy P. Tarcher, 2013).

Wilson, K. G. and Murrell, A. R., 'Values Work in Acceptance and Commitment Therapy', in Hayes, S. C., Follette, V. M. and Linehan, M. (eds), *Mindfulness & Acceptance: Expanding the Cognitive-behavioral Tradition* (Guilford Press, 2004).

Recommended further reading

Chopra, Deepak, *The Seven Spiritual Laws for Parents* (Crown Publications, 1997).

CHAPTER 5

Sources

Damasio, Antonio, *The Feeling of What Happens* (Mariner, 2000).

Bauer, E. P., LeDoux, J. E. and Nade, K., 'Fear Conditioning and LTP in the Lateral Amygdala Are Sensitive to the Same Stimulus Contingencies', *Nature Neuroscience*, vol. 4, no. 7 (2001).

Bishop, C. M., *Neural Networks for Pattern Recognition* (Oxford University Press, 1995).

Doidge, Norman, *The Brain that Changes Itself* (Penguin, 2007).

Dweck, C. S., *Mindset: The New Psychology of Success* (Random House, 2006).

Dweck, C. S. and Leggett, E. L., 'A Social-cognitive Approach to Motivation and Personality', *Psychological Review*, vol. 95, no. 2 (1988).

Hebb, Donald, *The Organization of Behaviour* (John Wiley & Sons, 1949).

LeDoux, Joseph, *The Emotional Brain* (Simon & Schuster, 1996).

Leggett, Ellen, 'Children's Entity and Incremental Theories of Intelligence', paper presented to the Eastern Psychological Association, Boston (1985).

Zull, James E., *The Art of Changing the Brain* (Stylus, 2002).

Zull, James E., 'The Art of Changing the Brain', *Educational Leadership*, vol. 62, no.1 (2004).

CHAPTER 6

Sources

Cahill, Larry, 'An Issue Whose Time Has Come: Sex/Gender Influences on Nervous System Function', *Journal of Neuroscience Research*, vol. 95, nos 1–2 (2017).

Clore, Gerald L., *Psychology and the Rationality of Emotion* (NCBI, 2017).

Damasio, Antonio, *The Feeling of What Happens* (Harcourt, 1999).

Damasio, Antonio, *Looking for Spinoza: Joy, Sorrow and the Feeling Brain* (Harcourt, 2003).

Franks, David D., 'The Neuroscience of Emotions', *Handbook of the Sociology of Emotions* (Springer, 2006).

Halpern, Diane F., *Sex Differences in Cognitive Abilities* (fourth edition, Psychology Press, 2012).

Hanson, Rick, *Hardwiring Happiness* (Rider, 2013).

LeDoux, Joseph, *The Emotional Brain* (Simon & Schuster, 1996).

Rollin McCraty, 'Heart–Brain Neurodynamics: The Making of Emotions', *Issues of the Heart: The Neuropsychotherapist*, special issue (2015).

Selye, Hans, *The Stress of Life* (McGraw-Hill, 1956; revised 1978).

Siegel, Daniel J., *Mindsight: The New Science of Personal Transformation* (Oneworld, 2010).

Chapter 7

Sources

Almon, Joan, *Adventure: The Value of Risk in Children's Play* (CreateSpace, 2013).

Brooks, Robert, *Raising Resilient Children* (McGraw-Hill Education, 2002).

The Child and Youth Well-Being Index (CWI), Center for Child and Family Policy, Duke University, Durham, North Carolina, http://www.soc.duke.edu/~cwi.

Harris, Angel L. and Robinson, Keith, *The Broken Compass* (Harvard University Press, 2014).

Levine, Madeline, *The Price of Privilege* (HarperCollins, 2006).

Liedloff, Jean, *The Continuum Concept* (Adlibris, 1975).

Maloney, Erin A., Ramirez Gerardo and Gunderson, Elizabeth A., 'Intergenerational Effects of Parents' Math Anxiety on Children's Math Achievement', *Psychological Science*, vol. 26, no. 9 (2015).

Rosenfeld, Alvin and Wise, Nicole, *The Over-scheduled Child: Avoiding the Hyper Parenting Trap* (St Martin's Griffin, 2001).

Rosin, Hanna, 'The Over-protected Kid', *Atlantic* (April 2014).

Sandseter, Ellen Beate Hansen, 'Scaryfunny: A Qualitative Study of Risky Play among Preschool Children', doctoral thesis (NTNU, 2010).

Shaw, Ben, Fagan-Watson, Ben, Redecker, Andreas et al., *Children's Independent Mobility: A Comparative Study in England and Germany (1971–2010)* (Policy Studies Institute, 2013).

Wilson, Penny, *The Playwork Primer* (Alliance for Childhood, 2009).

Young-Eisendrath, Polly, *The Self-Esteem Trap* (Little, Brown, 2009).

CHAPTER 8

Sources

Benor, Daniel J., 'Distant Healing', *Subtle Energies & Energy Medicine*, vol. 11, no. 3 (2000).

Covey, Stephen R., *The 7 Habits of Highly Effective People* (Simon & Schuster, 2004).

Easter, Alison, 'The Efficacy of Distance Healing Intentionality', research paper (University of Edinburgh, 2004).

Eisenberger, Naomi I. and Lieberman, Matthew D., 'Why it Hurts to Be Left Out', research paper (University of California, Dept of Psychology, 2004).

Lieberman, Matthew D., *Social: Why Our Brains Are Wired to Connect* (Penguin, 2014).

Mehrabian, Albert, *Nonverbal Communication* (Routledge, 2017: first published 1972).

Nichols, Michael P., *The Lost Art of Listening: How Learning to Listen Can Improve Relationships* (Guilford Press, 2009).

Pinney, Rachel, *Creative Listening* (The Women's Library Printed Collections, 1981).

Radin, Dean et al., 'Distant Healing Intention Therapies: An Overview of the Scientific Evidence', *Global Advances in Health and Medicine*, vol .4 supplement (2015).

Rosenberg, Marshall B., *Nonviolent Communication: A Language of Life* (Puddle Dancer Press, 2003).

Schlitz, Marilyn et al., 'Distant Healing of Surgical Wounds', *Explore*, vol. 8, no. 4 (2012).

Turkle, Sherry, *Alone Together: Why We Expect More from Technology and Less from Each Other* (Basic Books, 2011).

CHAPTER 9
Sources

James, P. D., *Time to Be in Earnest* (Faber & Faber, 1999).

Parra-Cardona, José Rubén et al., 'Epidemiological Research on Parent–Child Conflict in the United States', *PeerJ* (24 January 2017).

Qin Zhang, 'Family Communication Patterns and Conflict Styles in Chinese Parent–Child Relationships', *Communication Quarterly*, vol. 55, no. 1 (2007).

Siegel, Daniel J., *Brainstorm: The Power and Purpose of the Teenage Brain* (Jeremy P. Tarcher, 2013).

Singh, Rashmi and Kumar Nayak, Jogendra, 'Parent–Adolescent Conflict and Choice of Conflict Resolution Strategy', *International Journal of Conflict Management*, vol. 27, no. 1 (2016).

Recommended further reading

Taffel, Ron, *Childhood Unbound* (Free Press, 2009).

CHAPTER 10

Sources

Jung, Carl, *Collected Works: Vol. 17 – On the Development of Personality* (Princeton University Press, 1954).

Recommended further reading

Kabat-Zinn, Myla and Jon, *Everyday Blessings: Mindfulness for Parents* (Piatkus, 1997).

Acknowledgements

A book such as this is never just down to the work of its author but is the outcome of a host of influences, practices, trials and studies. Most important of all have been my experiences working with parents and children over these several past decades, and this book would never have come into being without them. I feel honoured and deeply grateful to have known each and every one of them. I am also immeasurably thankful for the invaluable work of the countless teachers whose work I have studied and integrated over the years, most especially my mentor, the late Kay Snow-Davis and the late Shakti Gawain from whom I first learned to trust my intuition. Both such great teachers, they are sorely missed. I also want to thank the Institute of HeartMath for unmatched and ongoing research into the significance of the heart and 'heart intelligence', which has greatly influenced my work.

On a more personal note, I am ever appreciative for the support, advice and wisdom of my colleagues Melissa Rivera and Tibisay Vera. To my agent, Fiona Spencer-Thomas, a special thank you for your 'stick-to-it-iveness'. Thank you also to the wonderful team at Robinson, especially Nikki Read and Giles Lewis for your faith in the whole concept of intuitive parenting. To Howard Watson a huge thank you for your skilful editing, making this book publishable.

Last but not least, my deepest gratitude goes to my daughter Tammy – for all your loving support and priceless feedback – and to my son-in-law Rory. This book is truly inspired by you both and your resolve to trust your parenting intuition and follow your north star.

Index